CONTENTS

S0-AYQ-845

Export Marketing for a Small Handicraft Business

Edward Millard

Oxfam/Intermediate Technology Publications

© Oxfam 1992

A catalogue record for this book is available from
the British Library.

ISBN 0 85598 174 1   Oxfam
ISBN 1 85339 106 9   Intermediate Technology Publications

Published by
Oxfam, 274 Banbury Road, Oxford OX2 7DZ
and
Intermediate Technology Publications,
103/5 Southampton Row, London WC1B 4HH

Designed by Jeffrey Meaton
Printed by Oxfam Print Unit
Typeset in Palatino 10.5pt

INTRODUCTION

During the last 25 years, Oxfam Trading has imported crafts from about 50 countries. This book has been written in order to share some of the experience we have gained. The number of producers around the world who want to sell their products overseas is far greater now than it was when we started. I hope the topics treated here will help them to think through the various aspects of export marketing, and learn from the examples of others — both how to do it and how not to do it!

This is not an exporter's manual. I have included the essentials of international trading procedures only briefly and generally. Rather, this is a book about how to reach, and respond effectively to, the overseas customer. Therefore, I hope it may also have something to offer the experienced exporter, as well as the less experienced ones for whom more will be new. A primary objective is that the material might be useful as a resource in training courses for export marketing. It may then be supplemented by reference to the specific procedures of the country in which the course is being held.

I have at the outset placed exporting in the context of an overall marketing strategy. It is Oxfam Trading's experience that many producers who want to export have not developed coherent plans, and analysed how they want to achieve them. Sometimes there are opportunities to sell more in their own countries. There is much common ground in good marketing practice, wherever the target customer is located. Many of the concepts in this book are applicable equally to domestic market promotion, and may assist some producers in increasing their success in that, too.

Most craft production units and marketing organisations are small-scale. They lack the sort of management structure, manufacturing adaptability, access to information, and financial strength which tends to be assumed in conventional textbooks about export marketing. I have tried to write throughout with their situation and perspective in mind, and discuss ideas which are realistic when working with limited resources.

My thanks are due to colleagues in Oxfam Trading who have commented on the text and especially to Maureen Clark, who typed it.

Edward Millard
Oxford, 1991

This book is intended to help producers of handicrafts extend their markets and increase their sales so that the people who make the products can receive a proper reward for their artistry and skill.

1 THE MARKETING MENTALITY

1.1 What is marketing?

Any sort of marketing is about four activities. They are commonly referred to as the four Ps:

Product, Price, Promotion and **Place.**[1]

They mean that successful marketing requires:

- offering a product which the market wants;
- selling it at a price which the market will accept;
- bringing it effectively to the market's attention;
- making it accessible to the market.

There is nothing in that list of activities to deter a small-scale business. They are all obvious enough. They can be summarised by saying that successful marketing requires knowledge of the market where you want to sell your product, and the capacity to respond to it. Any traditional artisan knows and carries out the four activities. For example, a maker of leather sandals in India knows what quality of sandal and what sizes the local people want; how much they are prepared to pay; whether they want them packaged, or offered on credit; and where they go to buy them.

The principles of export marketing are no different from this. However, if the four activities are looked at in more detail, then questions arise which cannot be answered easily by somebody without any export experience. Some of these would be:

Product

- Will customers overseas buy my existing product, or must I make something different?
- Are there other products like mine on the market?

1

- Do I need to make my product a different size, shape, or colour?
- What sort of quality standards do I need to meet, and are there any special regulations about this that I need to know of?

Price

- How much can I sell my product for?
- At what prices are similar products from other countries selling?
- Can I charge enough for my product to make a profit from exporting, given all the costs involved?
- Would the market in my own country pay more or less for my product?

Promotion

- How do I contact the overseas market?
- How much will it cost to promote my product overseas?
- How should I label and package my product?
- Which countries should I sell in?

Place

- Should I sell directly or through an exporter?
- Should I sell to importers, or shops, or agents?
- What documentation will I need for international shipping?
- Must the consignment be specially packed?

These questions, and others which might concern organisations wanting to export, fall into two categories. Some can be answered reasonably satisfactorily by **investigation**. For example, it is not excessively difficult to find out about documentation, or legislation governing international trade, or methods of payment. There are sources of information in every country. It is also possible to get answers to fairly specific questions about the overseas market. For example, what are the standard sizes for articles of clothing in the USA?

Yet many organisations who want to export their products do not ask these questions, nor get the answers, before approaching potential customers overseas. The reason is usually that they feel unsure about what and whom to ask.

More difficult to address is the second category of questions, answers to which require **judgement** or **experience**. For example, which products will sell overseas; at what price to sell in a market you do not know; what kind of packaging to use on your product — these are not things to which you can get factual answers. Some help is probably

2

closer at hand than most producers think. Smart shops in capital cities where crafts are sold are quite similar the world over. The sort of product presentation which is successful in Europe, for example, is much the same as in the well-to-do areas of the producing countries. Other questions can be clarified by careful analysis of the actual production situation. For example, the realistic range of product and packaging options depends on the capacity and skills of the producers, and the materials available.

Yet there is much that cannot be found out except by contact with the overseas market, and experience of dealing with it. Handicraft businesses which want to start exporting should follow two guiding principles: be **realistic**, and be **thorough** in your preparation. Being realistic means setting targets which you have a chance of achieving. It is invariably best to start modestly, and build slowly, learning as you go; and to contact as wide a range of potential customers as possible, because they will be your best source of information. Being thorough in your preparation means thinking of marketing not as a single aspect of a business, but as the whole approach to the business.

In carrying out the four activities which make up marketing, you are making the key decisions of the business. The other aspects — the material, human, physical and financial resources you need to run the business — are all in the service of creating the product, and locating the customer to buy it. Be clear at the outset that **marketing is not the same as selling**. Selling is trying to make the customer buy your products. Marketing is the process of finding out what customers will buy and then producing, promoting and distributing it at a profit. Thinking of marketing as the whole cycle of your activities means making it the basis of your business plans. You cannot make effective decisions about what to produce without thinking through the four marketing activities. You may not know all the answers to the questions, but you do need to identify the questions you want to ask, and how to find the answers. You must also think about how your business will have an income while you venture gently into the waters of export marketing.

Marketing is fundamentally a mentality: an attitude of mind. Any producer or trading organisation must be thinking constantly about what products to offer, and how and where to sell them. It is a circular process:

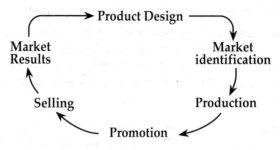

Fig. 1: *The marketing process*

Export marketing is really only the application of the Indian sandal maker's understanding of the local situation to a wider market place. If you want to export, you need information about that market place, and perhaps some guidance about effective ways of relating to it. That knowledge has then to be applied to your own situation and aspirations. To do that you will need the marketing mentality.

1.2   Analysing your options

Export marketing is only one option for the growth of a business. Many small handicraft businesses fail to undertake an analysis of other market opportunities which might present themselves. Many producers who have approached Oxfam Trading for orders have admitted that they have not really checked out new possibilities in their domestic market, nor thought of ways of selling more to their existing customers.

One writer on business management, H. Igor Ansoff, constructed what he called the Product-Market matrix:[2]

		Product	
		Present	**New**
Market	**Present**	Market penetration	Product development
	New	Market development	Diversification

Fig. 2: *Ansoff's Product-Market Matrix*

4

It illustrates the options for achieving business growth:

Market penetration: here you work within your present market in order to achieve better sales for your existing product range. An example would be an association of cloth printers who sell in their own country deciding to try to sell in different towns, or perhaps to hotels as well as retail shops.

Product development: the cloth printers might develop new products, such as bags or cushion covers, which they would try to sell to their existing customers.

Market development: the printers would offer their existing product, the cloth, to a new market, perhaps an export one.

Diversification: they might start up an additional, new activity for a new market.

A business might seek some combination of the four possibilities. It is for each business to decide its own plans for growth and development. It may be that exporting is the best or only realistic option, or indeed the basic reason for setting up the business. Conversely, it may be that exporting is not possible because production capacity is very small, or the production unit not very experienced commercially. The important point is that a business must **think through its options**, and then decide which products it is going to offer to which markets.

Many businesses say , 'We have a marketing problem'. The statement is often a cry for help, rather than an analysis of their situation. What they mean is, 'We want to sell more products', but there is no definite idea of which ones, how, where, or in what quantity. In other words, there is no overall plan. The right starting point for making a plan is **an analysis of your own situation**. With reference to the marketing activities and the matrix, write down all the possible options that might be available in order to increase sales of your products. For example:

- Contact new customers in your own country.
- Develop some new products.
- Study the competition.
- Train more people to make the most successful products.
- Find out about exporting.
- Review your costings and prices.

- Design some new packaging.
- Improve the quality of your finishing.

Possible solutions need thinking about in a lot of detail. Whether or not they are realistic will depend on your analysis of your own capacity, which should follow next. You need to consider:

- The availability and price stability of the materials used in the products you sell. Would you be able to cope with an increased demand?
- The availability of labour, its skills levels, and training needs. Could the producers increase their output, while maintaining quality standards?
- Tools and equipment used or maybe needed in any expansion.
- The ease with which the type of products you sell can be stored and transported.
- Your financial position and access to capital.
- Your level of commercial skills and experience.
- The interests of the group of people involved in the business.

The aim of this analysis is to identify three key aspects of your present situation:

- What can you try to achieve with your present resources?
- What would you like to achieve if you had more resources?
- How could you obtain the resources you need?

From here you can start to make realistic marketing plans. If you want to export, but lack knowledge of procedures, or access to finance, or production capacity, it would not be a realistic plan to start looking for overseas customers. Instead, you should try to find out how to export, and where to get finance, and work on your production. In the meantime, opportunities to sell should be sought nearer home.

You must develop a marketing mentality when making plans. Always think about where and how you will be trying to place your products before starting to produce them, or purchase them if you are a trader. Think first whether there are opportunities for penetration of the market you know already, perhaps with new products, or new prices or packaging, before you embark on the riskier voyage in search of new markets.

A small business might not aim to make the most profit, but make plans for reaching other goals. For example, production may be organised for the benefit of training everyone, rather than producing in the most efficient manner; or it may be limited in order to give more time to social programmes. It is up to each business to decide its objectives. **Analysis**, then deciding on a **plan of action**, must form the basis of any business activity, even if this is not oriented towards maximum growth and profit.

1.3   Domestic and overseas markets

Many times in response to the question, 'why do you want to export?' small handicraft businesses have answered, 'Because we cannot sell our products in our own country'. In fact, if a handicraft cannot be sold in the country of production, it is very unlikely that it can be sold anywhere else. In any market a product must fulfil the basic criteria of **acceptable design, reasonable quality**, and a **competitive price**. If it meets these to the satisfaction of the export market, then almost certainly there is also a market somewhere in the country of production. Few small handicraft businesses research those possibilities sufficiently. In Kenya, a basketry society out in the country complained of not being able to sell its products in the popular tourist centres of Nairobi and Mombasa. 'How often do you go there?' I asked. 'We do not bother any more', was the reply. Instead of giving up, the society should have analysed the information gained from its earlier visits to try to develop products which those markets might buy.

As a general rule, a business must never stop exploring possibilities of selling in its own country. The domestic market has many advantages over export:

- The business can understand it and make contact with it easily, so it is easier to respond to its requirements and produce the products it will buy.
- Prices to the consumer are lower. In export markets distribution costs add greatly to the final price.
- Orders can be fulfilled more quickly because the market is closer.
- It is simpler to service: no documentation, or export packing are required and there are no entry restrictions and customs duties.
- Payment should be quicker.
- The products are usually not subject to so much international competition as they would be in export markets.

7

The types of markets available will usually be various. It is common for a small business not to have explored them all. There are three main types of market: wholesale, retail and institutional:

Wholesale: The business sells not to the consumer, but to a retailer, exporter or other intermediary. This is often the only apparent option for small-scale producers, who cannot afford to have their own shop but who need a wider distribution than the local market place. The disadvantages are that handicraft traders in most producing countries pay poorly and often take goods only on consignment. By being out of touch with the actual consumer, you learn less about the market reaction, or about the price your product will bear.

Retail: A business can sell to the public directly in other ways than by having its own shop. It can sell from street stalls, in markets, and take part in specially organised fairs and exhibitions. These happen in all producing countries. They are very worthwhile for a business which usually sells wholesale, because they offer a chance to listen to comments from customers, and, of course, to sell for higher prices, too. The chief disadvantage in selling to the public in one locality is that the market is small and quickly becomes saturated, unless the area is a popular tourist spot.

Institutional: By this is meant selling to other businesses. An example would be hotels, who purchase handicrafts to decorate their rooms and lobby and sometimes to use in the dining room. Companies often need business gifts; handicrafts are appropriate because they can be individualised. Hospitals, railways and many other institutions may buy handicrafts.

To be satisfied that it is achieving most of the sales available to it in the domestic market, a business should check back on its list of possible solutions. Is it producing an adequate number of **new products** to satisfy its existing customers? Could it improve the **quality** or **presentation** of its products? Are there towns, or **types of market** it has not explored?

For example, a jewellery workshop for disabled people in Kenya had a steady market inside the country selling to other shops, and directly to tourists. The wholesale trade was not very profitable, largely because customers took so long to pay. So it built a new showroom and opened its workshop in order to encourage more tourists. It designed new items and also started up a garment workshop. It successfully increased its sales by this combination of market penetration and product development.

Domestic markets probably cannot absorb all the handicraft production seeking an outlet. Compared to overseas markets, they have three main disadvantages:

- They are usually not large. Populations may be small, and disposable income levels low. Many producing countries report falling demand, as economic difficulties reduce people's purchasing power.
- The artisan sector is often viewed disparagingly in producing countries by well-to-do people, who tend to prefer industrial products, often imported. As a result, reliance on tourism is often strong.
- Prices obtainable in the domestic market may be very low because of the excess of production capacity over demand, and the competition from products serving a similar purpose.

Overseas markets, despite their remoteness and difficulties, provide a great stimulus to new product development. Governments often provide a financial incentive to exporters, because they earn foreign currency for the country, and provide employment opportunities. **Export markets offer an important outlet for handicrafts, and should be pursued, though within an overall marketing plan which looks at all the options for business growth.**

Summary

1 Marketing is the process of finding out what customers will buy, and then producing, promoting and distributing it at a profit. The results determine how you proceed in this continuous cycle of activity.

2 Business growth can be achieved by developing either production or promotion or both. A business must make realistic plans based on an analysis of its own situation and capacity.

3 The domestic market has a number of advantages over the export market, although it also has some disadvantages. It should always be investigated thoroughly for sales potential.

2 THE BUSINESS APPROACH

2.1 Alternatives for exporting

If a small handicraft business has decided to include exporting in its marketing plan then it is faced with a choice. It could export directly itself or through another organisation. Many small businesses do in fact produce for overseas markets without undertaking the exporting procedure. Sometimes they are unaware of the final destination; they simply sell to a trader. Often, though, they do know to whom their products are being sold, but they have chosen not to export directly.

Handicraft production units are of numerous types. The main ones are:

- a self-managing group of producers — for example, a co-operative, association, union, or informal group;
- a group which is not self-managing — for example a project in which the activities are controlled by an agency (church or voluntary organisation, whether local or foreign);
- a privately-owned workshop, with employer-employee relationships;
- a workshop run by local or central government.

Any of these may choose to export directly. In order to do so they will need:

- fulfilment of local legal requirements (registration, export licence or similar);
- the commercial knowledge to locate and respond to overseas customers by undertaking the marketing activities;
- a sufficient level of organisational and financial strength to fulfil export orders.

Many handicraft production units cannot meet these three criteria. A great deal of production in the sector takes place on an informal basis, by individuals, families or small groups. They are producers rather than business people, whose only option is to sell in small quantities to traders. Private traders are not the only type of export marketing organisation. Many governments — in some countries local as well as national — have set up handicraft-marketing organisations. Additionally, in some countries, there are what are called alternative trading organisations. The objective of these is to offer marketing and other services to producers, to assist them in the distribution of their products and in strengthening themselves as businesses. Such marketing organisations might be established by voluntary agencies, or by groups of production units themselves.

In order to decide whether to export directly or through a trading organisation, a production unit should look at the **advantages and disadvantages** of the two options. The advantages of direct exporting are fairly clear:

- You are paid directly by the customer instead of having to wait for payment to be passed on to you by the exporter; this applies also to any advances paid.
- You would benefit from any export incentives (rebates, duty drawbacks) provided by the government in order to encourage exporters. These could amount to a good deal of money over and above the income from the sale of the actual products.
- The contact with the market is direct; you control your own destiny. Another production unit, which makes similar items, may get an order through the trading organisation which you might have been able to get yourself, directly from the customer.
- Less quantifiably, the direct contact with the market overseas provides you with vital market information and new ideas. There is no substitute for communication with the customers.

On the other hand, a trading organisation can often fulfil a vital role where a production unit wants to sell overseas but not directly. There may be some good reasons for choosing this distribution option:

- Production capacity may be quite small and the quantity of goods not sufficient to be exported. This is very common, because so many handicrafts are produced in family workshops. Traders often purchase the same product from many different production units, thereby collecting an exportable quantity.
- The amount of production destined for the export market may be so low that it is not worthwhile to get embroiled in the bureaucracy of export procedures. Some production units make this decision because the majority of their sales are in the domestic market.

- The production unit may be too distant from a city where the export formalities would need to be completed.
- There may be an alternative trading organisation which offers a very supportive and favourable relationship.
- The production unit may not be confident enough to take on exporting.
- Exceptionally, there may be logistical, or even legal, impediments to obtaining an export registration. A refugee group, or an organisation politically unacceptable to the government, may encounter such problems.

Many businesses are too weak financially and commercially to export directly. It is often also much more cost-effective to organise distribution to a central point in the producing country, and then make a single large export consignment. The question in this sort of distribution structure is **whether or not the producer is getting a fair deal.**

Anybody involved in the handicraft business knows that, in the majority of cases, producers are not fairly rewarded when they sell their products through intermediary marketing organisations. Their lack of knowledge about who stands in the distribution chain and at what price their product is finally exported, and their lack of other market options, oblige them to accept very low payment from profit-motivated traders.

For this reason, it is usually worthwhile for a production unit to think carefully whether or not it could take on direct exporting. Lack of confidence is a major problem. Many small businesses have put up a mental barrier against exporting, as if it were an abstruse science, too difficult to understand. They should take heart from a group of just six people in Zaire, who set up a small production unit to make clothing in the home of one of them, called *Action pour la jeune fille*. They succeeded in making their first export consignment to Oxfam Trading in 1990. In a country where supplies and communications are difficult, and bureaucracy demanding, they managed to print cloth labels and buy plastic bags as we requested, and obtain the documents they needed in order to send the goods out and allow us to import them into Britain. The process cost them much time and anxiety, but they were rewarded with a feeling of considerable achievement — and also another order.

Some producers have perfectly satisfactory relationships with an exporting organisation, although rarely, it must be said, with governmental ones. To assume that all private exporters treat producers unfairly would be wrong. Some exporters, who are open about their relationships with the producers, will invite prospective customers to visit the production units.

A few private trading organisations, with a genuine interest in the welfare of the producers, offer them additional benefits beyond a fair price: perhaps training, or medical or other benefits. Such concerns about the welfare of the producers are a fundamental characteristic of the alternative trading organisations (ATOs). Oxfam Trading buys from many of these. One such is *Asociacion Aj Quen* in Guatemala. It is a membership organisation of some 35 producer groups in the country, who elect the Council of Management. This employs specialist staff to manage the business on a daily basis and to work with the 2,500 artisans who belong to the member groups. *Aj Quen's* objectives are to seek new markets and fair prices for its members; to offer them credit facilities; to provide technical assistance and product development training; to strengthen organisational structures so that efficiency is increased and groups acquire management skills; and to promote Guatemala's cultural heritage. It covers the costs of the commercial activities through a mark-up on the products, while covering the social programmes through outside funding.

ATOs have different activities and some will emphasise social development programmes more than others. Production units should not assume that ATOs are necessarily their best option. We have heard a number of criticisms about different ATOs over the years:

- They might not be well connected in the export market. By relying on them, you will not undertake your own export promotion; yet you might not receive many orders.
- Other groups making similar products to yours may be supplying the same exporter, and so competing with you for any orders.
- They might not in fact trade as fairly as they should. Some ATOs are slow payers.
- They concentrate most of their effort on production units whose products sell best, rather than help to strengthen the weaker ones.

The options which a production unit has for the export of its products should be regularly reviewed, like all business arrangements. Oxfam Trading met a group of women lacemakers in south India, who were selling all their production to an exporter in Delhi, the capital. We found a market in Britain for their work, and as a result the women were able to double their daily wage rate. Such dramatic examples are rare, but in general, anywhere in the world, ignorance will always tend to be exploited. The best negotiating position is always knowledge — of the market value of your product, and of export procedures. Then at least the exporter will know that you know what should be happening.

Oxfam Trading states as one of its basic objectives the empowerment of small-scale handicraft producers. We aim to support their efforts to earn more money and improve the quality of their lives. We believe that the prerequisite for this to occur is a process of organisation among producers, to counter their isolation and lack of confidence, and enable them to learn together. In making business decisions which are based on understanding the marketing process, a small-scale production unit will be able to pursue its commercial interests more effectively and develop the human potential of its members more fully.

2.2   A marketing plan

Planning means deciding what you are going to do and how you are going to do it. The marketing plan is concerned with the objectives of the business, and the activities to be undertaken in pursuit of them. It could be set down under two headings:

Strategic objectives: these are the basic aims of the business, not spelt out in detail, but comprehensive. A small handicraft co-operative selling in the domestic (local and capital city) market, but wanting to export so that it can grow, might set down its strategic objectives for the coming year as:

- To expand membership by 20 per cent by maintaining our existing rural and urban markets, and by opening up export markets in Europe.
- To begin a savings scheme for members.

Operational activities: this is the more detailed part of the planning process, in which a business decides which activities it needs to undertake to achieve the strategic objectives. The co-operative might, for example, plan:

- To develop a range of approximately 15 new products in the first six months, concentrating on easily transportable items. (Design group)
- To introduce new quality control systems. (All members)
- To appoint a sales representative in the second half of the year, responsible for domestic and export customer contact. (Management committee)
- To get information about overseas markets from banks, government offices and shipping agents. (President)

- To talk regularly to local community groups about our activities. (Secretary)
- To talk to a bank next year about starting a savings scheme. (Treasurer)
- To review performance and adjust targets accordingly every six months. (All members)

Plans should have time scales attached to them. The strategic objectives should cover perhaps a three-year period. The operational activities should include a **target time** by which they should be achieved. They should also **allocate responsibility** to a person or people who will undertake them.

Planning is not something which a business does once, at the start of its life; it should do it continually. Like the marketing process, it is a circular activity:

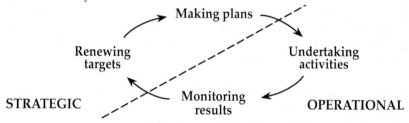

Fig.3: *The planning process*

Plans must be constantly reviewed in the light of what happens, so that they remain achievable. They must be expressed in terms which can be **measured**, and against which activities can be defined. For example, a strategy to 'start exporting' would be too vague. If in two years' time you had achieved one export order, it would seem to fulfil the stated objective and the marketing manager might claim to be successful, but you might actually be disappointed with the performance. Again, if you do not state where to export to, how can you target your promotion? It would be much better to set a strategic aim 'to start exporting in Europe next year'. This could then be followed up by a statement under operational activities 'to make a three-week visit to Scandinavia and Germany in the autumn'.

Regrettably, many small-scale handicraft businesses do not make marketing plans. As a result they adopt a passive approach to marketing, probably maintaining the existing customer base, but getting new sales only when an actual or potential customer makes an enquiry. Even if they succeed in getting orders, they may have difficulties in production, or in fulfilling export procedures. To plan means to adopt a **business approach** to your activities: to think about your options, decide your best course of action, and organise yourself to undertake it. It is a dynamic process, in which you are looking for your customers and ensuring you have the capacity to respond to them. You do not have to be a big business in order to plan; but if you do not plan, you almost certainly never will be one!

Business, of course, is unpredictable and you cannot plan for everything. New market opportunities might occur which you had not foreseen, such as a fashion craze in Europe. Conversely, a supply of raw material might dry up because of a change in the weather. Nor can you plan down to the last detail. If you are entering new fields of activity, such as an export market, you cannot possibly predict all you will need to do and know in order to obtain and fulfil orders. This is why **planning is a continuous process**, in which you should always be analysing what has happened in the past in order to estimate what is likely to happen in the future.

For example, analysing your sales performance is a vital activity. If certain products are not selling well, you need to ask why; ask yourself and, if possible, ask your customers. Look at the products against your better sellers. This will help you identify the direction in which your product range should be moving. Did your performance deteriorate: late deliveries, poor quality, perhaps? A marketing plan is the application of the marketing process to your particular situation.

Planning must start with knowledge — or at least an informed guess — about the markets in which you are going to sell. You cannot say, 'Because we make baskets, we will sell 1,000 baskets this year'. What you can say — provided you have a reason to believe it — is, 'Because the market will buy 1,000 of our baskets this year, that is what we will produce'. From the identification of the market opportunity and a decision about the products to offer, you must then consider the other aspects of the marketing process — your pricing policy, means of promotion and method of distribution. The decisions which you make provide the plan.

The more experience you gain, the easier it will be to make realistic plans. The more realistic they are, the more rigorously applied and the more carefully they are assessed, the better chance you have of achieving your objectives. Without a marketing mentality, you are unlikely to make good plans. There is always more than one option throughout the marketing process. Consider the various possibilities of attracting customers for 1,000 baskets. You might make baskets of the highest quality and seek a high price, or sell them more quickly and cheaply because a particular market is very price conscious. You might like to use the opportunity to train some new producers. You might decide to take a sample to a new market to see if you can get some new customers. The decisions you make will be the ones which appear to serve your aims best.

Many small handicraft businesses adopt a product-oriented rather than market-oriented approach to their activities. This means that they make their key decisions about what to produce, and at what price to sell it, without analysing the market opportunity or thinking about the options available in the marketing process. They try to sell what they can produce, rather than try to produce what they can sell. They are more influenced by tradition and a fear of risk than by the realities of the market place, and as a result their chance of acceptance in the market is less. They are going against the law of business, which says that **production exists in order to satisfy demand**, not to satisfy producers.

It is of particular concern in the handicraft sector that many product-oriented businesses have been established by agencies wishing to promote income-generation activities. They have often been set up without prior reference to market opportunities for what is produced, and lack a flexible approach to pricing and promotion.[3]

For example, in southern India, a project was begun by an agency to produce a range of palm-leaf bags, hats and place mats. The objective was to provide work for 25 women in the community. Palm leaf was the only locally available raw material. A designer was recruited, who taught the women how to make the products. A grant was made by a foreign agency for the training and initial production, and items of a reasonable quality were produced. Costs were calculated, and selling prices set to provide a profit margin of 10 per cent, which would represent the women's income. It was assumed that a market would be available in the cities, and it was hoped that contact could be made with overseas customers too. Within a year the group had disbanded, for lack of a market. An attempt had been made to contact outlets in some cities, but the prices offered were below that required to yield a profit. A few letters were written overseas, but with no response.

This sort of story is unfortunately very common. It results in a lost investment by the agency, and disappointed hopes on the part of the producers. What had gone wrong was:

- The agency did not research the marketing options. It made wrong assumptions about what could be sold.
- There was no attempt to find potential customers for other types of palm-leaf items (such as brief cases, linen baskets, shopping baskets).

- The local market was already saturated with similar items from other producers.
- The responsibility for making contact with potential customers had not been clearly allocated.

It cannot be said that the project would have succeeded with better planning. Ultimately a business can succeed **only if a market is available** for products it can offer. Perhaps the group had no real chance of selling palm-leaf products. The project could have increased its chances of success, and lessened the adverse consequences of failure, by more systematic market-oriented planning. It should have investigated more carefully the potential markets for palm-leaf products and considered the possibility of other types of production. It should have started more modestly with just a few producers and a smaller investment. Objectives and activities should have been fully discussed and agreed with the producers, and frequently reviewed and adjusted in the light of experience. The project, in short, had been conceived without a marketing mentality, and established without a business approach.

These fundamental requirements can be summarised as follows:

Marketing mentality: this recognises that marketing success depends on a dynamic relationship with the market, in which the product is adapted to the requirements of the market. The process starts with the market, not with the product.

Business approach: this establishes systematic planning and monitoring procedures so that activities are always based on realistic objectives.

When making your plans, ensure that:

- they are achievable;
- the whole organisation is committed to them;
- people are allocated to the key tasks;
- there is a time-scale for the activities;
- the objectives can be measured;
- you have thought of all the things you need to do or find out in order to try to achieve them;
- you have thought about the resources you will need in order to achieve them;
- they will produce the results which you want.

The credibility of a business depends to a large extent on the quality of its planning, and rightly so. Why, for example, should a bank finance additional production if there is not a realistic plan to sell it? Oxfam Trading is often asked to provide financial support to print an export catalogue. Before we consider such requests, we always ask where this activity fits into the overall marketing plan. Is this really what is required, or might there be other, better ways of achieving the strategic objective of gaining new overseas customers? Is there a plan to distribute the catalogues? Are there people who are able to follow up enquiries? Without a comprehensive plan, no bank or agency will have the confidence to support a small-scale business.

2.3   Researching the market

Most small handicraft businesses which have not yet started exporting feel daunted by their ignorance of overseas markets. Before you approach a customer, you must plan the type of offer you are going to make as a result of your analysis of your situation and the information you are able to gain about the market into which you are offering your products.

There are two key decisions to be made: **what products** should you offer to overseas markets and into **which markets** should you offer them?

The more information which can be found out before making plans, the more achievable those plans can be, and the less money and energy will be wasted on false hopes. To say that experience is the best guide is not a lot of help to organisations which want to export for the first time. Nor are the marketing textbooks which advise market research through consultancy studies or visits to the target market. These are usually too expensive for a small handicraft business.

There are many ways of acquiring information about overseas markets. The starting point is to make a list of what you want to know, and what can be found out. Market research must always seek information which is obtainable, and relevant. For example, it would be pointless for a carpet exporter to try to find out the relative quantities of carpet imports in three different countries. That information would hardly assist a decision as to which one of the three would be most interested in the exporter's particular type of carpet.

The most important information which is obtainable and relevant for export marketing is:

Distribution structures: An understanding of how an overseas market is structured will enable an exporter to target potential customers. For example, it is no use contacting a retail shop overseas if it is not an importer.

Cultural, economic and climatic factors: These can all influence customer behaviour. For example, you would not be very successful selling grass mats whose use — for sleeping on — is tied to the culture of the producing country and which would have no use in the country where you are hoping to sell them.

Legal considerations: There may be rules and regulations governing the importation of the products you want to sell — perhaps there are restrictions, special documents, duties, quality standards or labels.

International trade procedures: There are various procedures concerning shipping and forwarding, documentation and payment.

Assistance programmes for exporters: There may be credit schemes, or export incentives available and there may well also be help in locating and contacting customers overseas.

All of these should be researched at least to some extent before embarking on export marketing. Like your plan, your preparation is what gives you credibility. If you seek an order overseas but do not actually know how to send a consignment out of your country, you are not going to give a very favourable impression to your potential customer.

There are a number of different sources of information in countries which produce handicrafts. The availability of these varies greatly from country to country, and it will be necessary to travel to the capital city to contact them all. The main ones are:

Central government offices: Every country has a body responsible for export promotion. It would usually be found within the Ministry of Commerce or Trade. Most handicraft-producing countries also have a crafts promotion body. A few countries in which handicrafts are an important export, for example India and Mexico, also have regional offices for export crafts promotion.

Government offices ought to be able to answer most of your market research questions, especially those to do with assistance programmes to exporters and international trade procedures. They are often much less knowledgeable about other aspects of overseas markets.

Information may also be scattered in different ministries. Handicraft promotion can interest government departments responsible for culture and tourism, as well as industry and commerce. There are several countries in which a department for crafts promotion exists in two or three or even four different ministries.

Banks: They can tell you about international payment methods.

Shipping and forwarding agents: They can provide all the necessary information about export documentation and transportation services.

A local Chamber of Commerce or trade association: They may have some information which could save more arduous investigation in the capital city. Libraries will provide general country information.

Embassies of foreign countries: They could assist with contacts in their country.

International agencies, and foreign voluntary agencies: They may have offices in your country and provide information and contacts.

All of these sources of information would be available to a small handicraft business without a contact overseas. Yet rarely have would-be exporters done all that they could to inform themselves about their chances.

There is another very valuable source of information which is available to a would-be exporter. This is observation. Everybody is a consumer, and capable of analysing their own reactions to products on sale. By studying what sort of things attract you to a product, you can start to think about what might attract customers to your products.

Unfortunately, certain very important aspects of overseas markets are not realistically researchable by a small handicraft business. The two big questions are the **level of competition** and, related to that, the **choice of country or type of customer**. Unless you visit a country, or have contacts who can give you good information about it, you cannot hope to learn much about products similar to yours which might be available to your potential customer. This vital information is only gained by experience. You might be able to find something out about other exporting organisations in your own country, but nothing about what is coming from other countries. This large hole in export market research capacity is sufficient reason to limit your ambitions, and the allocation of resources, in the early stages of exporting.

You should also consider whether or not there are potential export markets near to your country. Given two markets willing to pay an equal price for your product, the closer of the two would always be your better option. This is because you would find it quicker and cheaper to fulfil orders, and easier to visit. There is no better way to learn about overseas markets than to visit them. This is how you get a real understanding of their structures, and about competing products.

There is a certain amount of regional trade in handicrafts. The existence of a large tourist market in a country will inevitably attract handicrafts from nearby countries. Sometimes handicrafts bear the name of the country in which they are being marketed, even though they were made elsewhere. It seems perhaps dishonest, but is it really any different from labelling a product with your customer's brand-name?

One criterion, then, for the choice of country in which to promote your products should be **proximity**. Most small businesses would know, or could find out, whether important markets for handicrafts exist in nearby countries. A second criterion might be the **coherence** of the area. For example, it would not make much sense to select, say, USA and Germany as two possible export markets. USA and Canada, or Germany and Netherlands would be a more logical choice, because of the possibility of visiting both countries on one business trip; and also because there are some similarities between the markets of neighbouring countries, so that the learning process becomes easier.

Personal or organisational interest, or contacts, might be criteria for selection of countries. An export organisation which receives some funding support from a foreign agency would logically seek markets in that country.

As a general rule, as in all business ventures, it is best to **start in a limited way** by selecting only a small number of countries in which to test your products in the first instance. If the products are not accepted, do not immediately jump to the conclusion that you picked the wrong countries. It may be that the same outcome would await you elsewhere, and that what you have to do is look at your products again.

There is another general rule to remember: **always relate any business venture to your own interests and capacity;** or to put this in business terms, do not undertake activities which do not match your plans and resources. If you could not cope with a large increase in orders, do not go out and seek one.

2.4 Matching resources to plans

Even the most carefully researched and prepared marketing plan will succeed only if resources are made available to carry it out. These resources are of four types:

Material

You must ensure that you have adequate access to raw materials and labour to fulfil orders. In Oxfam Trading we have frequently been let down by suppliers because of a shortage of materials. Of course, it might have been unforeseeable that a shortage would occur after an order has been accepted. Still, you must do everything possible to find alternative sources of supply in case the unforeseen actually happens. In business, it is always worthwhile to have what we call 'contingency plans': an alternative course of action if something goes wrong. For example, we placed an order for a drum from an alternative trading organisation in Africa. We promoted it in our catalogue, but it was not supplied. We were informed by the supplier that the carver of the wooden stem had a personal difficulty which kept him off work for two months. Nobody else could do the carving. The supplier had not got a contingency plan, and was unwise to offer for export a product whose production depended on a single person.

Supplies must be guaranteed for making not only the product, but also the packaging. We ordered a musical instrument from Mexico which was suitable for children, but not for very young children, and we asked for a label to be applied stating that. The supplier replied that they were unable to print labels and did not know where to get them made. This could have been found out very easily in the local community. To be able to respond to reasonable, normal requests for labels and packaging from overseas customers is part of the necessary preparation for export.

Human

Probably the greatest weakness of small handicraft businesses throughout the world is their management capacity. This is not surprising; most producers are not business people by tradition or inclination. They understand the product and its production method. They have much less experience of the rest of the marketing process: promotion, distribution and even pricing. They struggle to find a market because they do not know how best to price, promote and place their product. It is certainly true to say that much of the beautiful craftwork still being produced is not yielding its real market worth, because it is not marketed in the right way.

A common problem is dependence on a single person who heads the organisation. Even in organisations which are democratically structured, with responsibilities clearly divided up between members or partners, this difficulty can occur. It is not so much a question of structure, but the competence which may be acquired from experience or good training. It is unlikely that a single person can deal adequately with every aspect of the complex activities involved in managing an export handicraft business. Most organisations concentrate by necessity on either the promotional aspect, or the production, or the human relationships with the producers. Organisations which adopt a business approach to the whole marketing process, while at the same time pursuing the welfare of the producers, are the exception. We have some suppliers whose social programmes are excellent, but whose customer service is poor. Others are the opposite, and although they offer an excellent service, we are aware of difficulties in their relationships with the producers.

People allocated to the key tasks in the marketing plan must be willing and competent and also have the time to undertake them. Otherwise, the tasks will not be done. Human beings like to organise themselves, rather than be organised. If a manager wants to commit an employee to a task, it is a much better approach to discuss it with the person than to issue an order that it be done. The employee must feel a personal commitment in order to undertake the task dynamically; otherwise it will probably be done to a lower standard. People need not only **motivation** to perform business tasks competently, but **training**. A training plan should be part of the activities of every business. For example, does the person who will be responsible for contacting customers overseas know the procedures for export?

Production skills are seldom lacking. Oxfam Trading's experience is that relatively too much money tends to be invested in production rather than in management training. Of course, a business which seeks to increase its sales must ensure that there are adequate numbers of skilled producers. Also, there should be a constant effort to upgrade skills, or perhaps introduce new techniques or technology. The jump from domestic to export marketing may require training related to the standards necessary in the new markets.

Physical

By this is meant the equipment, workshop space or storage capacity that a business might need in order to grow. It is a requirement which

Oxfam Trading understands well. Our own growth over the years has led to significantly increased stockholding levels, which in turn has caused us to acquire more warehouse space. Many handicraft products are extremely bulky, especially as we now include furniture in our product range.

Equipment can improve production efficiency. The introduction of small-scale technology — for example, a wood-sander, a spinning wheel, a leather stitching machine, a temperature-controlled kiln — can not only increase output but also improve quality, and reduce production costs. A production unit should know what equipment is available, and judge at what stage in its development it would be appropriate to acquire some.

Financial

All plans must be looked at financially. Two questions should be uppermost in your mind:

- What will be the financial consequences of the plans we have made?
- What financial resources shall we need in order to undertake our plans?

It is through adding the financial consideration that the marketing plan becomes an overall business plan.

A business needs to prepare two financial projections as part of its planning. A **profit and loss** (or income) statement will estimate the financial results of the activities it plans. For example, suppose a small production unit selling hand-printed textiles in the domestic market decides to try to open a market in the neighbouring country where there are increasing numbers of foreign tourists. It has heard from people who have been there that some private traders from that country are already buying similar textiles and selling them at a large profit. While maintaining all the current activities which secure its domestic market, it decides on the following new ones:

- It will produce an additional quantity of its usual product range during the first four months of the year.
- The Chairwoman and another member will make a visit to the neighbouring country in June for two weeks in order to contact potential customers.
- It will try to sell the products at a higher price than it usually gets in the domestic market. It usually adds a mark-up of 25 per cent, but for this trip will add 40 per cent.

The production unit estimates that with luck it might sell three-quarters of the products, which can be carried by the two visitors. The rest would be sold on the domestic market as usual. Production will be reduced evenly over the rest of the year to absorb the surplus. It then writes down its financial projection. This includes the regular domestic trade, but the new venture is itemised separately so that members can understand it easily. The period of forecast should be at least one year.[4]

Projected Profit and Loss Statement 1992

	Domestic	Export	Total
Sales	25,000	2,520	27,520
Less: cost of sales	20,000	1,800	21,800
(labour and materials)			
Gross profit	5,000	720	5,720
Less: overheads	3,000	750	3,750
Net profit	2,000	(30)	1,970

Fig 4: *Textile production unit: financial projection 1*

The cost of undertaking the export promotion trip is estimated to turn the venture into a very slight loss unless sales exceed expectation. Nevertheless, it is agreed by the members that it is a sound plan because opportunities in the domestic market for growth are very limited, and there are a number of skilled women in the community who would like to join the group if there were more work available. If the trip is successful, then in future it could be undertaken more cheaply by just one person, and the stock carried would be matched more closely to the market's requirement.

The projected financial performance serves as the vital check at the planning stage that the plan is realistic: the unit is profitable enough to risk a small loss. In the worst eventuality, if it sold nothing overseas, its overall income statement would look like this:

Gross profit	5,000
Overheads	3,750
Net profit	1,250

The venture is low risk because the production can anyway be sold on the domestic market.

The profit and loss statement is also the basis for review during the year of how performance is matching up to plans. It is from the comparison of performance with plans that the business knows when to take corrective action in the present, and for the future how to adjust its plans and allocate its resources in the most effective manner. For example, the Textile Production Unit might decide that it is sufficiently profitable to start up a new training scheme, or lower its selling prices in the hope of being able to employ more people. It must always know what its financial position is, and what the financial consequences of its actions will be.

If profit is what enables a business to grow, cash is what keeps it alive on a daily basis. A business needs to make a second financial projection in its plans, which is a **cash-flow statement**. This shows when and to what level cash resources will be needed in the business in order to achieve the plan.

The Textile Production Unit plans to have a total income in 1992 of 27,520, and total expense of 25,550, yielding a profit of 1,970. A cash-flow statement sets out in monthly detail at what time the revenue will come in to the business and the expenditure go out. This essential information enables it to ascertain if it will need to go to a bank for short-term finance, or perhaps if there will be times of surplus when money could be invested profitably. The cash-flow statement also includes any other expenditure, such as purchases of capital items. These are not treated in the profit and loss statement, which is basically a trading account — but they have to be paid for.

For example, the Unit needs to buy two new sewing machines in 1992, costing 500 each. It estimates they will have a life of five years, and so it has allowed for a depreciation cost of 200 in the overheads indicated in its profit and loss statement. However, the cash expenditure will be the whole 1,000. The Unit sells on an average of 30 days' credit, but pays wages and material suppliers in the same month as production. Domestic sales are evenly spread January-October and there are none at all in November or December, when the Unit closes each year. It will bear 280 overheads each month for electricity, water and miscellaneous equipment.

Projected Cash-Flow Statement 1992

	Jan	Feb	Mar	Apr	May	June	July	Aug	Sept	Oct	Nov	Dec
Receipts												
Sales revenue		2500	2500	2500	2500	5020	2500	2500	2500	2500	2500	
Payments												
Production	2600	2600	2600	2600	2000	2000	1850	1850	1850	1850		
Overheads	280	280	280	280	280	280	280	280	280	280		
Export trip					750							
Fixed assets				1000								
Total expenditure	2880	2880	2880	2880	3280	3030	2130	2130	2130	2130		
Net Cash	(2880)	(380)	(380)	(380)	(780)	1990	370	370	370	370	2500	

Fig 5: *Textile production unit: financial projection 2*

The Unit now knows how its planned activities will affect not only its profitability, but also its cash situation. The statement shows clearly the effect of receiving sales revenue one month after making production expenditure, and of the additional call on cash which the early-year export production makes. It shows the fundamental importance of cash; the Unit is planning a profitable venture, but for five months will have a negative cash balance. Unless it has accumulated some capital in the past, or has access to borrowing, it will not actually survive to make the profit.

If the trading profit of 1,970 is realised, it would be accounted for as:

Profit available for distribution and reserves	1170
Transferred to capital account	800
	1970

When making financial plans, remember three things:

Add a margin of safety: Some planned sales may not actually be achieved; some customers might not pay when they are supposed to. Your plan should identify the maximum funding requirement you could need, so that you could take steps to cover this.

Include selling expenses: It is a common error for small businesses to overlook the costs of promotion. The consequence may be that you cannot then afford to undertake the activities needed to sell your products. There can be no rule as to how much a business should spend on promotion, but it is unlikely you will spend much less than 10 per cent of sales turnover, if you are giving the selling effort the attention it needs. It might be spent in different ways — such as recruiting a sales manager, making an overseas visit, producing a catalogue, exhibiting in a fair. Do not make the mistake of thinking that the customers will find you; they will not, or anyway not enough of them.

The cost of money: Exporting usually means enduring a considerable delay in the receipt of payments. In several producing countries, banks are slow in processing international payments. There can be long delays between incurring production expenditure and receiving sales revenue. This can adversely affect the cash flow of a business, and also its profitability. For example, if a business borrows money at 20 per cent per annum and sales revenue takes three months to arrive in its bank account, its costs have effectively increased by 5 per cent.

Financial projections provide the information necessary to make realistic action plans. Unless each stage of planning is expressed in financial terms, you cannot be sure that cash exists to carry plans out, or that the resulting gain or loss to the business is an acceptable result of undertaking them.

Summary

1 A handicraft business wishing to export does not have to do it directly. It may choose to work through an exporter. Alternative trading organisations (ATOs) can offer a range of commercial and social services to organised producer groups.

2 Planning is essential to the success of a business. Plans must be realistic, have the agreement of everybody involved in implementing them, include a time for achieving them and allocate responsibilities to people for carrying them out. Planning must be based on past performance and future possibilities in the market place.

3 Careful preparation must be made for an export marketing venture. Find out as much as you can about your target markets from sources of information available in your country. Make a small and coherent selection of countries to approach in the first instance.

4 A business must ensure that it has the material, human, physical and financial resources required to implement its plans. It needs to make financial projections of its profit and its cash flow in order to ensure it can remain operational.

3 MARKETS AND THEIR CHARACTERISTICS

3.1 The perception of value

'There is ... no such thing as a "market". People talk about the Swiss market or the American market, but they do not exist ... so I suggest you forgo using the word "market" and think first in terms of customers and then the countries where they happen to be.[5] This good advice might help to break down a little of the mental barrier which would-be exporters instinctively put up against overseas markets. Markets in every country have a great deal of diversity. In a typical handicraft producing country the range of different markets might be something like: the local village market place; the rural or small town shop; the smart large town or capital city shop; tourist stalls and shops; a fair or exhibition; museum or gallery shops; a trading organisation; and an export company. All of these might be places where a production unit could sell its products. The price obtainable, or the requirements about quality or packaging, might be different for the same product, depending on which market it chose.

The situation in the countries which import most handicrafts is much the same. In Britain, Oxfam Trading has a chain of shops. Because these are located all over the country, it might be assumed that we sell to most of the country's markets. This is not the case. Markets are differentiated not so much by geography as by income levels and attitudes of the customers. Of course, these can have something to do with geographical location; an area in which most of the people are poor will not have shops selling very expensive products. However, in most areas in Britain, there are people of all income levels. So you cannot really talk about 'the market in London'. There is smart London, where rich people shop, and street-market London, where most of the customers are on low incomes. Marketing people often speak of 'going upmarket' — meaning targeting their products to well-off customers — or 'downmarket' — to ones less well-off.

Markets are defined according to the **type of customers** who use them. For example, an alternative trading organisation wants to export baskets made by a tribal group. These are of functional shape, commonly used by people in the domestic market as bowls for fruit or bread. What is distinctive about them is their form of decoration, employing natural dyes, and using symbols which have meaning in the culture of the community. The tribal group has an established price which is calculated loosely on its estimation of their production costs.

The ATO must choose how to offer the product, with the objective of making the maximum profit. It has to decide at what price to offer it, how to promote it, and where to place it in the market. What it wants to find out is how to give the baskets their highest possible **market value**.

The price which a customer is prepared to pay for a product has little to do with the cost of production. Think about the things you buy yourself: do you know how much they cost to produce? Not normally. What you do know is how much they are worth to you. Customers buy products which are offered in a way which corresponds to the value they are prepared to give them.

Value is the price at which a product can be sold. It will vary according to the way in which the ATO undertakes the marketing process. There are several ways in which it could increase the value of the baskets:

Quality of manufacture: customers might be prepared to pay more for items of high-quality production.

Promotion of decorative qualities: the ATO would seek to stress the beauty rather than the function of the baskets in its presentation, offering them as works of art rather than fruit bowls.

Providing information about the product: in this case, information about the cultural significance of the design might be produced on a high-quality label.

Targeting the promotion at specialist outlets: there are high-class shops or galleries where customers are seeking distinctive original products of artistic merit.

The value of products depends partly on where they are sold. In a specialist, 'upmarket' shop like this, customers are prepared to pay high prices for distinctive artistic products. Tumi, Oxford.

In other words, the value of the baskets would depend on how they were presented to which market, and where the ATO was successful in placing them. The quality of production, promotion and presentation of the product, and the skill at placing it, will affect the price which the seller can obtain. **Value derives from the total offer,** not just the product itself.

It follows that changing one aspect of the offer will affect other aspects. Oxfam Trading sells through Oxfam's shops and through a mail-order catalogue. In the catalogue it is possible to achieve a higher quality of presentation, because products are professionally photographed, often in display settings. As a result, we can often obtain a higher price than would be possible in our shops, where space is limited for display. Conversely, we would probably be more successful selling a woollen rug in our shops, where customers could feel the quality. In a photograph it would look similar to a cotton or acrylic rug, and this might adversely affect its value. The presentation of products through packaging and display is called **merchandising,** and it clearly influences consumers in their buying decisions.

Value is a concept which varies according to the nature of the particular market into which a product is placed. For some, variation in a design may have value because the product is unique; for others it may imply imperfection compared to an industrial product. A specialist outlet requiring individual, culturally interesting products

33

might accord value to an original musical instrument. For other markets its value may be low because people do not know how to play it.

The same consumer will often make two different buying decisions in two different market places. A good example is the **tourist market**. When people travel to a new place, they generally like to buy some souvenirs, for themselves or as gifts. They tend to shop much less carefully than they would at home, and to accept lower quality. The fact that the product is made locally is the important factor. The same product on sale in their own country would usually have less appeal. It would be more expensive because of distribution costs, and the consumer would not normally be looking for a product from a particular country. Tourist markets are generally a poor guide to buying habits in the countries from which those tourists come.

If there are rational reasons why consumers accord value to products, there are also a number of less tangible ones, such as: [6]

distinctiveness
emulation of others
pride in their personal appearance
pride in the appearance of their property
association with social achievement
expression of artistic taste
ambition
romantic interest
maintaining health
cleanliness
proper care of their children
satisfaction of appetite
pleasing the sense of taste
securing personal comfort
alleviating laborious tasks
security from danger
pleasure of recreation

While not all of these may be applicable to handicrafts, the list serves to emphasise that consumers have a **very wide variety of motivations**, and accord value to products for all sorts of reasons. That understanding was well captured by the head of Revlon Inc., a North

American cosmetics manufacturer, who said, 'In the factory we make cosmetics. In the store we sell hope.'[7]

It is also worth noting that people often buy things simply because they enjoy shopping! Market research in Europe has indicated that up to 25 per cent of people go shopping as a leisure activity. They may well choose to buy a product because they are just relaxed and happy.

Two aspects of the offer which cannot usually be included in a list of consumer motivations are how and where the product was made. As consumers, we know that we are not often interested in whether a product is made by hand or machine, or in which country. The only occasion on which these factors have importance is where they give additional value to the product. If hand manufacture can achieve a quality which a machine cannot, then it will have more value; if the quality is the same, the value is the same. The place of origin of a product may have value for a customer with an interest in a particular country, but most will be only concerned about quality, design, price and presentation.

There is a further factor to which markets accord value. This is the **quality of service**. The best offer in the world is worthless if ultimately the contract is not fulfilled. Exporters must be very clear about the expectations of customers which they themselves have created. Like the other aspects of the total offer to the customer, service is a variable. An exporter may choose to offer certain special services — for example, free samples, documents sent by courier, best quality packing materials — and recover the cost by edging prices upwards. Alternatively, cheaper but less reliable forwarding agents might be selected in order to keep the price down. Service may be the single point of differentiation between exporters who are trying to sell the same product into the same market. For example, in Kerala, in southern India, coconut matting is exported in large quantities at fixed prices set by the state government. Given that the product quality is strictly controlled, it is only in the quality of service offered to the customer that one exporter may claim superiority over others.

The combination of the various aspects of the offer — the product, its price, promotion and placing on the market — and the service to the customer together comprise what is called the **marketing mix**. The marketing process can be seen as the attempt to convert a capacity to produce into a marketing mix of the highest possible value.

3.2   Competition

In this marketing process, an exporter's offer stands alongside offers by others, with which it is in competition. Successful marketing means creating a marketing mix which is better than one's competitors. **Competition can apply to all aspects of the mix**: a better-designed product, a cheaper price, more effective promotion, a more receptive market place. Many handicraft exporters already know that different aspects of competitiveness appeal to different markets. In general, if selling 'downmarket', it might be worth sacrificing quality in order to achieve a cheaper price than others. Conversely, in a market particularly appreciative of high quality, it might not matter that your price is higher than your competitor, if your product is superior in finish.

Robert Davis/Oxfam

The Rwandan basket sells for six times as much as the set of four baskets from Bangladesh. If your products cannot compete on price, they must compete on quality and distinctiveness.

Inexperienced exporters tend to focus wrongly on price as the single factor in competitiveness. In fact, it is the **best value** which customers seek, and in determining value they take into consideration the whole **marketing mix**. If this were not the case, how would anybody sell basketware from anywhere but South-East Asia, which generally has the cheapest baskets? Other countries are able to compete, not on price, but on quality and distinctiveness of design, because many customers accord value to those factors. Producers find great difficulty in appreciating how distinctive their products may be in another country, and hence what value they might have.

Promotion is another vital aspect of the marketing process. Having competitive products is not enough if you cannot bring them effectively to the customer's attention. For many would-be handicraft exporters, this is a critical weakness. They would be wise to spend more on promotion, even at the expense of price increases to cover the costs of it. Price is, after all, the easiest aspect of the marketing mix for competitors to attack. Much less easy for them to beat is your quality of production or promotion. It is certainly true that many exporters succeed with not very competitive product ranges because they promote them very effectively. Competition is intense in the handicraft trade. It comes not only from similar products elsewhere — **direct competition** — but also from other products which may serve the same purpose — **indirect competition**.

Direct competition is the easier to confront because it is more easily understood. If you are an exporter of painted *papier mâché* boxes from Kashmir, it is fairly clear that you are in competition with other exporters of the same items. But you are also in competition with exporters of painted boxes from other countries, such as Thailand and Haiti. These may be made from wood or bamboo, but the finished product is very similar. A great difficulty facing exporters is how to know what other products similar to theirs are available to the customers to whom they are trying to sell. This is a strong reason in favour of making a visit to a country to which you want to export.

Products are generally valued according to the **purpose** for which they are made. **Purpose is not to be confused with function**; the purpose may be to produce something purely decorative. Objects which are not particularly functional, but have special decorative qualities, might have a very high value. The purpose of a painted *papier mâché* box may be said to be both functional — to contain things, and decorative — to look attractive. Its value derives from both considerations. It is worth more than an undecorated box of a similar size or than a similar piece of painted *papier mâché* which is not a box. Of the two purposes, it is possible to have a clearer idea about the value of its function than the value of its decoration. A box of a certain size may have an approximate value in a particular market; customers might be looking for the cheapest box which is available to perform that function. It is much more difficult to estimate how much decorative qualities are worth. Clearly, an exceptionally beautifully decorated box, perhaps painted with gold leaf, is worth more than a routinely decorated one. The value of decoration ultimately depends on the price particular customers in a market place are willing to pay for it, and it is much more difficult to assess what that might be without experience.

It follows that competition is always strongest where products are valued primarily according to their function. If you offer a simple undecorated box, there will almost certainly be many other similar boxes on the market. The competition to a decorated box is less strong because the box has been **differentiated** from others available in the market place and has gained an additional value directly related to its decorative qualities.

Competition with handicrafts comes not only from **similar** products from other countries, but also directly and indirectly from industry. Direct competition occurs when manual techniques are replaced by mechanical ones: hand-looms by power-looms for example. The production of a piece of cloth by machine at a lower cost reduces the value of the similar piece made by hand. Industry also competes indirectly with handicrafts by the production of items serving a similar purpose. Many traditional crafts all over the world are being displaced by the introduction of new products made by machine. The plastic bucket which performs the same function as the ceramic pot reduces the value of the pot to less than that of the bucket, which has the additionally valued quality of being light to carry. Cheap plastic and rubber sandals have put traditional cobblers out of business, because many customers in the markets in which the shoes are sold do not accord a higher value to hand-stitched leather sandals, which cost more to produce.

The only weapon available to handicraft producers to fight industrial competition is the **enhancement of value through decoration**. Oxfam Trading is able to sell, for example, lampshades and picture-frames made by hand. They are more expensive than ones sold in other shops, made by machine, but they sell because our customers accord value to their decoration. It is industry's capacity to respond to people's functional requirements by producing more cheaply which obliges handicraft production increasingly to emphasise decorative qualities. It is here that distinctiveness can be created, and additional value gained. The artisan who produces purely functional items with little or no decoration will be struggling to earn a living wage.

It is because the value of handicrafts lies to a considerable degree in their decorative qualities that market research is of limited usefulness. Research can most effectively survey competition to products where value is related almost exclusively to function. Exporters of leather bags would gain little help from a survey of the British market for bags. All it would reveal is that there are many types of bags — leather, fabric, plastic and others — at all prices.

Indirect competition hits much more widely than exporters usually assume, because everything is in competition for the money which a customer is disposed to spend. Sometimes customers are quite specific in their requirements. For example, if they want to buy a cushion cover, they will not spend the money on anything else. At other times, customers are much less definite in their requirements. They may be looking for an item of clothing, but not sure whether to buy a jacket, a jumper, or a pair of shoes. Or they might want something to decorate a wall. It could be a woven tapestry, a wooden carving, a painting, or even a large basket. So a tapestry might be in competition with a basket for the same amount of money.

This sort of customer behaviour is much more pronounced when buying **gifts for other people**. Very often, at Christmas time for example, shoppers set out with a certain sum of money, and a list of people, but no clear ideas as to what to buy for whom. The patterns of customer behaviour at consumer level are always mirrored in the trade by the professional buyers. When Oxfam Trading is putting its range of products together, we know that we want a certain quantity of specific products — some clothing, furnishings, rugs, etc. However, we are flexible about the precise quantity and type of each; and also about what other types of products we shall include. Our final selection depends on which products we think offer the best value. If we see four good jumpers, we might buy them. If we see only two, we might buy two more items of brassware or stone carvings as well.

Competition extends very widely. Perhaps the only comfort is that not even the most detailed and expensive research will reveal it all to you. Experience and understanding are the best guides: to know not only which of your products sell well, but why. The only practical advice can be to **concentrate on what you are good at**, and not to lose business to competitors by a shortfall in your own marketing mix which you could very well have overcome.

3.3 Market structures

Understanding the customer's psychology increases the chances of success in marketing, but first you have to find the customer. To do this, you have to look in the right place. All markets have **structures** which are defined by the functions they perform in the distribution of products. So, retailing is a market structure which distributes products to consumers; whereas the function of wholesaling is to distribute them to retailers. Exporters need to understand at what level in the structure the potential customers who might actually buy from them are to be found. Otherwise, they might waste money targeting their promotion at the wrong people.

Hence, it is not an adequate marketing strategy to say, for example, 'I am going to aim for the fashion market', or 'the tourist market'. You first need to know what the point of entry is into these markets for an exporter, according to their structures.

The structures are not the same in all markets, but follow a common pattern, which has evolved in order to distribute products profitably. The total **distribution chain** in handicrafts starts and finishes with a single person (or family) — the producer and the consumer. For the products to be moved from producers to consumers cost-effectively, they need to be handled in large quantities. In the case of export, they also need to be shipped to the country of destination in large quantities. A lorry or a container usually costs the same to hire, whether you fill them completely or only to half capacity. A typical distribution pattern for export is therefore something like this:

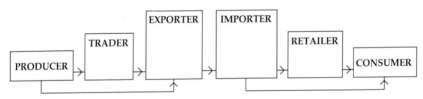

Fig. 6: *Distribution structure in the handicraft trade*

The functions of the distributors in the producing and the selling countries are exactly inverse. The local trader is bulking up for efficient export; the retailer is breaking down for selling to the individual consumer.

Because **handling adds cost**, it is in the interests of both producers and consumers that the distribution chain is kept short. In the producing countries it can be reduced if the producer sells directly to the exporter. The producer and exporter are both likely to earn more if the goods do not pass through other traders. Sometimes producers can join together to form their own export organisation. This might add only a small mark-up to cover the cost of handling and shipping the goods, leaving a greater benefit for the producer. Oxfam Trading buys from several exporting organisations which belong to the actual producers — co-operatives, associations or unions.

However, the usual situation is that the producers are not able to export directly — for lack of production capacity, organisation, knowledge about procedures, working capital and contact with overseas markets. They therefore sell to traders, though, of course, they may also sell directly to the public in their domestic markets. Nor is it always only one trader who stands between the producer and exporter. The goods may be bought and sold by two or more people before they finally reach the exporter. In such cases, the remuneration to the producer is usually very low. This is why many ATOs encourage producers to organise together in some way, in order to shorten the distribution chain.

In the country of sale, variations in the length of the chain also occur. Exceptionally, a wholesaler might stand between the importer and retailer. Wholesaling as a function has lost much of its former importance. This is because retail businesses have grown bigger, and are able to buy in larger quantities. Some are big enough to act as importers themselves, so that the goods pass directly from the importer to the consumer. Oxfam Trading is one example of this shortest possible distribution structure in the country of sale.

Retailing is to be thought of as a **function** — that of selling to the consumer — and not necessarily as a location, i.e. a shop. There are five main types of retailing organisation:

- a single shop or boutique;
- a group, which has branches of the same shop in different towns;
- a trader who sells in a street market or from stalls;
- a mail-order business;
- a business which sells through local representatives, who organise informal sales in people's houses or perhaps in church halls. (This is sometimes called 'party-plan selling'.) In Britain, Traidcraft is an example of an organisation which imports handicrafts and achieves a high percentage of its sales in this way.

Mail-order is an increasingly popular way of selling handicrafts. In Europe it has about 15 per cent of the retail market, so it is still much less important than shops. The business produces a catalogue containing photographs of its product range, with descriptions, dimensions and prices. It mails the catalogue to its existing customers and other potential buyers. The customer sends an order together with the money, and the company sends the products, usually by post. Unlike the other retailing methods, there is no opportunity for the customer to see the actual product before purchasing. This consideration, and the payment in advance, seem strange to many exporters: why do consumers like to purchase by mail-order? The reasons have to do with lifestyles, and alternatives. The advantages of buying through a mail-order catalogue in Britain, for example, might be:

- Most shops close at the same time as people come out of offices, and are also closed on Sundays. Saturday is a popular shopping day, but many people work then, or are engaged in sporting or other activities.
- Women are increasingly working similar hours to men, and so also have little time to shop.
- Parking cars is difficult and expensive in town centres, where most shops are found.
- With the growth of retail groups, there are fewer small individual shops, so the consumer has less choice. Mail-order catalogues may have unusual products.
- There is very little choice available in shops to people who live some distance from towns. Oxfam Trading's catalogue, for example, is very successful in rural areas.
- People who have little mobility, perhaps because they are old or disabled, or have childcare responsibilities, find it convenient to shop from home.
- Mail-order businesses offer money-back guarantees, and accept credit cards, so that the consumer risks nothing and can defer payment.

The exporter's potential customer might be a retail group, a mail-order company, or an importer who does not sell direct to consumers. It is the **capacity to import** which matters to the exporter. It is no use promoting your goods to a retailer who buys only from importers.

Knowing where to look for your customer means also going into the right **trade segment**. Markets define products by their purpose, not by their method of manufacture. Hence 'handicrafts' is not a marketing term. There are few importers who buy the whole range of products which are commonly offered by exporters of handicrafts, because there is such a great diversity of products. Oxfam Trading classifies its handicraft product range according to the following product types:

Product group description	Products within group
Furniture and storage	Linen baskets
	Wastepaper baskets
	Picnic baskets and hampers

	Cabinets
	Bookcases and shelves
	Tables
	Chairs and stools
	Magazine racks
	Mirrors
	Trays
Household	Baskets
	Bowls and dishes
	Kitchen equipment
	Tea towels
	Aprons
	Tea cosies and oven gloves
	Crockery and cutlery
	Dusters, brushes and brooms
	Tablemats
Candles and incense	Candles
	Incense
	Holders
Furnishing textiles	Wallhangings
	Hanging tidies
	Cushion covers
	Bedcovers
	Floorcoverings
	Table linen
Decor and ornamental	Hanging baskets
	Mobiles
	Boxes and containers
	Figurines and carvings
	Pictures
	Photograph frames
	Lamps
Clothing	Skirts and dresses
	Trousers
	Jumpers and cardigans
	Blouses and shirts
	Jackets
	Dressing gowns
	Scarves
	Gloves
	Hats
	Belts
Accessories	Wallets and purses
	Bags and luggage
	Footwear

	Sandals
	Slippers
Jewellery	Bangles and bracelets
	Necklaces and pendants
	Earrings
	Brooches
	Rings
Toys and hobbies	Puzzles
	Games
	Toys
	Dolls
	Musical instruments
Garden	Garden clothing
	Planters and vases
	Garden utensils
	Hammocks
	Garden furniture
Stationery	Writing paper and notelets
	Wrapping paper
	Stationery racks
	Pen trays
Greetings cards	Handmade cards
Christmas sundries	Christmas decorations
	Calendars

Markets in the countries which import most handicrafts are specialised. The importer who buys basketry will probably not buy jewellery. This is because consumers want to see a good selection of the particular product which they intend to buy. People going shopping for a carpet generally go to a specialist carpet shop which will offer a large range from which to choose. The person responsible for buying for the carpet shop will need to know the carpet trade well in order to stock the shop properly. It is easier to be successful by specialising, because you can become expert at what you do, and make your selection more attractive to consumers. General importers who try to cover a very diverse product range, as Oxfam Trading does, find it extremely difficult to be knowledgeable and successful in all of it. We do it because we have a particular interest in supporting as many types of handicraft producers as possible.

Exporters of handicrafts need to identify into which trade segment their particular products fall, and then approach this at the correct distribution level. The product will be categorised by the market according to its purpose. The importers may often also trade in products within their segment which are made by machine. This would almost certainly be the case with carpets, for example.

This very practical issue of how a market place is actually organised, and hence who the potential customers are, is difficult for new exporters to research adequately. Each country will be a little different. The chances of understanding will be greater if you **limit the number of countries in which you try to sell**, so that you can visit each country and gradually get to know its markets better.

3.4   The costs of distribution

As products pass through the distribution chain from producer to consumer they bear **costs**. Consider a purchase by Oxfam Trading of alpaca sweaters from Peru. We buy from a Peruvian ATO which works with women's groups in the countryside. Between the producer and the consumer (our customer) the following costs will be added to the product:

PRODUCER'S SELLING PRICE	=	PRODUCTION COST PLUS PROFIT
Labels and bags		Each jumper must have a sewn-in cloth label and be sold in a plastic bag.
Internal transport		To the exporter's warehouse in the capital city.
Export packing		Strong quality cartons.
Export formalities		Transport to port or airport, preparation of documents and clearance through customs by a forwarding agent.
Exporter's charges		For services to organisation of production, quality control, packing and undertaking export, plus profit.
Overseas transport		To country of destination.
Customs clearance		In country of destination by a clearing agent.
Internal transport		To importer's warehouse.

Insurance	Throughout the journey.
Storage and distribution	In warehouse and to shops or mail-order customers.
Tax	Jumpers bear 17.5% Value Added Tax in Britain.
OXFAM TRADING'S SELLING PRICE =	**PRODUCER'S SELLING PRICE PLUS DISTRIBUTION COSTS PLUS PROFIT.**

There could be variations in this list of distribution costs. Some countries levy **taxes on exports**. This would be one more cost. Most handicrafts enter Britain without being subject to **duty**. Some clothing items bear duty, although not usually hand-knitted jumpers. There are a considerable number of costs, and these will be applied even in the shortest distribution chain. When additional traders enter the picture, there are further handling costs and profits for the products to bear.

Who is going to bear these costs, the exporter or the importer? It is an important question, because misunderstanding often occurs in an export contract, causing an argument about whose responsibility it is to pay certain costs. The answer is that it depends on the **terms of the contract**. It must be made absolutely clear between exporter and importer when making a contract precisely which costs are included in the price quoted.

The distribution chart can be simplified by amalgamating certain costs, as shown in Figure 7.

PRODUCT (including labelling, packaging and packing)	INTERNAL TRANSPORT AND EXPORT FORMALITIES	INTERNATIONAL SHIPPING (including insurance)	CUSTOMS AND DISTRIBUTION COSTS IN COUNTRY OF SALE
1	2	3	4

Fig. 7: *Export distribution*

The price which an exporter quotes could be based on assuming responsibility for costs in Box 1, or 1 + 2, or 1 + 2 + 3. It would never include those in Box 4. There are terms to describe these three different ways of quoting export prices:

Product including labels, packaging and packing	=	EX WORKS
Above plus internal transport and export formalities	=	FREE ON BOARD (FOB)
Above plus international shippingand insurance	=	COST INSURANCE FREIGHT (CIF)

(There are other possibilities, but they are not commonly used.) In the handicraft trade, the majority of prices are quoted on the basis of either ex works or FOB. This means that the importer has the responsibility to pay for the costs of international shipping and insurance.

FOB is the basis for pricing which most suits the importer. This is because the importer knows how much the product is actually costing when it leaves the country of origin. With an ex works basis of pricing, the importer can have some nasty surprises. Oxfam Trading frequently does. For example, we imported some palm leaf picnic baskets from southern India. They had to travel from the production centre inland to the port. Because they were very bulky, several lorries were required, and we collected a bill for several hundred pounds. We had not realised transport would cost so much when calculating our own selling prices, and consequently we lost money. Moreover, how could we know if the exporter negotiated the best possible rate? It is a very trusting importer who agrees to pay charges over which no control can be exercised, nor the amount be known before shipment. Few importers will therefore feel happy about ex works prices.

However, for inexperienced exporters, ex works is the most favourable basis of pricing. They know how much it costs to produce the product, but have little knowledge about the costs of local transport or export formalities. If the importer insists that they quote an FOB price, they are worried that if they underestimate the costs, the contract will be loss-making; whereas if they overestimate them, their prices may become uncompetitive.

It is advisable for exporters to move towards an FOB basis of export pricing as soon as they can. Most exporters calculate from their experience the average of the costs in Box 2 as a percentage of their sales. They then add this percentage to the ex works price. It might be that on some consignments the actual costs are higher or lower than the amount allowed, but over a period it should average out about right. If not, they need to review the percentage added in the light of the latest bills.

Many of Oxfam Trading's difficulties with exporters occur when there is misunderstanding of what the terms mean. This is why **the**

details should always be spelt out in a new trading relationship. Many exporters have quoted us prices on an FOB basis and then sent us an invoice which adds some charges incurred in the country of origin, or the cost of sending documents by courier. FOB should mean that the importer incurs no costs until the consignment leaves the country of origin.

We once had a difficulty with an exporter in Kenya who quoted us FOB prices and subsequently sent us an invoice for local transport costs, and additional packing. When we queried it, the explanation came back that the basis of FOB was to send the goods by air freight from the capital city, Nairobi, which is inland. As we had requested sea freight, additional transport was needed to send the consignment to the port, Mombasa, and extra packing for better protection. This was reasonable enough, but we explained that the price list should then state clearly FOB Nairobi, packed for air freight, so that the customer would be prepared for the additional cost if sea freight was used.

We have had similar misunderstandings with exporters over the meaning of ex works. It is usually taken to mean that **the product is labelled, packaged and packed for export**, and that only the costs of internal transport and export formalities are omitted. Nevertheless, we have received bills for printing labels and even for plastic bags and packing.

In Figures 8 and 9, typical price movements are shown in the total export distribution process. It is difficult to generalise about costs of transport for handicrafts. There are very large variations according to which type of products are being exported from which country to which. Oxfam Trading's average input costs are not 23 per cent, but less than 20 per cent. Transport, however, is not the largest distribution cost; that is incurred in the country of sale. In the example given, a product landing in an importer's warehouse in Britain at £1.60 would be sold to a consumer at over £5.00, five times more than the producer received for making it, and about four times more than its FOB price. This is not untypical. As a rule of thumb, importers think in terms of FOB x 4 as the final selling price when deciding whether or not to take an interest in a product. When we make our buying decisions in Oxfam Trading, we estimate costs rather more precisely according to the actual type and origin of the product. However, if I am selecting samples while visiting an exporter, FOB x 4 is my guide. If I think the product could not sell in Britain for four times its export price, it is unlikely that I would select the sample.

The explanation for the large increase in price within the country of sale is the high cost of living there. The major costs are: rent of warehouse, rent of retail premises or publication of catalogue, fixtures and fittings, staff wages, heating and lighting, packing materials, transport, interest and promotional materials. Employers also incur costs for staff benefits, such as medical schemes and pensions. Additionally, there will be a profit for the wholesaler and retailer, and a sales tax. The costs of retailing are higher than wholesaling because distribution is in smaller quantities, so that more space and staff are required to sell the products. Where the wholesaler and retailer are the same, then the overall costs can be reduced, but not by very much. Most of the same functions still have to be performed, except wholesale selling.

In order to recover these costs, we need to add the sort of mark-up to the products we buy which is shown in Figure 9. For expensive products we may add a smaller percentage. Most handicrafts are of relatively low value, and many are of large volume. To import, store and distribute laundry baskets, for example, not only incurs high costs of transport, but also takes up a considerable amount of expensively rented warehouse space. Even on products which we can import and store cheaply, it is extremely unusual for us to sell at less than three times the FOB price.

The procedures and costs of international distribution are poorly understood by many handicraft exporters, and especially small, inexperienced businesses. But it is very important to understand them. How can you be effectively engaged in the export business, and give good service to the customer, if you do not know the procedures for making the consignment arrive safely and cost-effectively in your customer's country?

The export-import procedure, as described in Boxes 2, 3 and 4 of Figure 7 comprises:

- export formalities: the procedure by which the exporting country regulates all exports;
- international freight;
- import formalities: the procedure by which the importing country regulates all imports.

The costs of the export and import formalities are only partly related to the size and value of the consignment. There are **minimum charges** whatever the size. Hence the cost of these as a percentage of the consignment's value is larger for smaller consignments, and smaller for larger consignments.

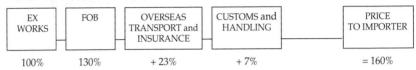

Fig. 8: *Composition of FOB price*

PRICE MOVEMENT FROM PRODUCER TO IMPORTER

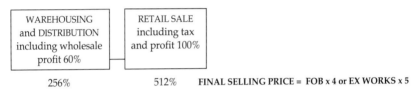

PRICE MOVEMENT FROM IMPORTER TO CONSUMER

WAREHOUSING and DISTRIBUTION including wholesale profit 60%	RETAIL SALE including tax and profit 100%
256%	512% **FINAL SELLING PRICE = FOB x 4 or EX WORKS x 5**

Fig. 9: *Price movement in international distribution*

Summary

1 Customers are not interested in what a product costs, but in what its value is. Value depends on the way a product is presented to a particular market. There are many different types of markets, and many different motivations for a customer to buy a product. The marketing process can be seen as realising the highest possible value out of a capacity to produce.

2 Product design, quality of production and presentation, the price of the product, its method of promotion, distribution, and the level of service to the customer are all variable factors in the marketing process. It is the way in which they are combined which defines what is called the marketing mix. All markets are competitive. Successful marketing means creating a marketing mix which is better than your competitors.

3 Markets are structured according to the function played in the distribution chain, and the type of product being sold. An exporter must identify the correct point of entry, in order to reach a potential customer. Making a visit to the target country will greatly assist identification of who the customers might be.

4 Distribution adds cost. When countries import handicrafts, they sell them at around four times the export price, in order to recover their costs, such as shipping, rent of premises, and staff. There are standard methods of pricing for export contracts, determined by whether the exporter or importer is responsible for certain of the distribution costs.

4   REACHING YOUR CUSTOMER

4.1   Means of communication

Exporters may come into contact with importers through one or more of six main methods: buying tours by the importer, correspondence, selling tours by the exporter, participation in trade fairs, overseas representation, merchandising houses.

Buying tours by the importer

This is Oxfam Trading's usual method, but is in fact fairly uncommon in the handicraft trade. We like to visit our suppliers because of our particular interest in knowing what type of organisation they have. Most importers are interested only in the exporter's offer, and do not necessarily have much to gain from visiting the source of supply. Overseas buying tours are expensive, and time-consuming. They are particularly difficult for a small business, where perhaps the buyer is also the owner, and needs to spend a good deal of time in day-to-day management of the business. They are also difficult where an importer buys from many countries. It might perhaps be possible to visit the most important from time to time, but not all of them.

An exporting business has a better chance of receiving a visit from an actual or potential customer if it is located in or near the capital city. Importers who make buying tours work to tight schedules, and may well spend less than a week in a country. This allows very little time to make contact with an exporter located in the countryside.

No exporting business can prosper by relying on buyers to seek it out. **It is for the exporter to take the initiative in looking for potential customers**. Many small handicraft businesses who want to export are insufficiently dynamic in doing this. They feel confused by the planning and research needed to contact custmers, and as a result do very little. A more aggressive exporter, perhaps with an inferior offer, may then get the business.

Correspondence

International trading relationships can be carried on quite successfully for long periods of time without the buyer and seller meeting. Many start by correspondence, again usually at the exporter's initiative. For most small handicraft businesses, it is the only realistic option, at least in the early stages of seeking export markets, when they are trying to **make contacts** and **gain information**.

However, correspondence is generally a very limited vehicle. The large majority of letters written by exporters to potential new customers are not answered by the importers. If the information given in the letter does not offer an importer the possibility of getting access to something new and interesting, then there is no reason to spend time and money writing back to the exporter. Oxfam Trading receives many letters from hopeful exporters who have researched potential customers in Britain and found our name and address. We reply to most of them, but as the majority come from private traders from whom we are not interested in buying, we write a short, negative letter. The types of small businesses which we would like to support are much less active in writing to us. When they do, we write back in some detail, specifying the further information which we would like.

Even when correspondence yields a response from an importer, it is likely to be no more than a request for further details of the exporter's offer. If this is to be communicated by further correspondence, then the exporter needs some **sales literature** to send. If none is available, the initial effort of making contact by correspondence was probably not worthwhile. If it is, then the relationship might proceed further with a request for **samples**. Buyers rarely commit themselves to orders on the basis of written descriptions or photographs. They are not so trusting as consumers who buy from mail order catalogues, because the consumers buy only a small number of items and can easily return them.

The usual process for buying without physical contact between an exporter and importer is:

Correspondence ——> Catalogue ——> Samples

Even when there is an actual meeting, this is likely to yield nothing more than a request for samples by the importer. When making overseas visits, many buyers do not make commitments for actual stock orders.

Selling tours by the exporter

This is usually the most fruitful approach to export promotion. It is probably essential to make an overseas tour if a small business is to make a significant impact in overseas markets. A visit by an exporter to the market place enables not only **personal contacts** to be made with potential customers, but also knowledge and information to be obtained about market structures, trade segments and competition. A day spent looking in shops can be tremendously instructive about what other products are available like yours, price levels, and methods of presentation.

In order to undertake a selling tour overseas, an exporter needs to have the resources to do it. A major problem is that the countries which buy most handicrafts are very expensive to visit. Human resources are needed, as well as financial ones. There must be a person competent and confident enough to travel to meet buyers in their own countries. It is the lack of resources which prevents most small handicraft businesses from taking the step. That being said, Oxfam Trading receives a great many visits from suppliers. All seem to agree that it is the most productive means of communicating with customers, actual and potential; and that in a few weeks much more can be learnt than in a year of correspondence.

To be effective, and especially cost-effective, a selling tour must be **carefully targeted**. You need to know which markets you are aiming for. It is often sensible to wait some time before planning to go overseas, and spend the initial stages of export promotion in investigating widely different types of markets, and narrowing down your options by information gained from research and reactions to correspondence.

Participation in trade fairs

There are an enormous number of trade fairs. They take place in almost all countries, mostly organised according to the trade segments into which the market divides products. Thus there would be fairs for jewellery, other fairs for carpets and still others for fashion. An important category is gifts, which is clearly a very wide one, in so far as almost any product could be classified as a gift. Some handicraft exporters have found them useful, especially as all of their product range can be offered for sale, which may not be the case in a fair for a more specialist market segment.

Trade fairs **bring together buyers and sellers** in a single centre, very often a purpose-built exhibition hall. In Britain, there is a National Exhibition Centre near the city of Birmingham. Each February a gift fair is organised there which attracts exhibitors from all over the world. Trade fairs are very attractive to buyers. They are able to see, all in one place, a large number of actual and potential suppliers. It is a very

Trade Promotion Services Ltd/Post Studios Ltd

Trade fairs, such as this one in Birmingham, can be useful to would-be exporters. They offer an opportunity to meet importers who may decide to buy your products.

efficient way to see the offers available to them. Fairs can also be attractive to sellers, for the similar reason that they can meet many buyers in a short space of time at a single place. Each company participating in the fair rents a space, which is called the exhibitor's stand.

However, **a fair must be very carefully chosen**. Many exporters have gone to a great deal of effort and expense to send their samples and attend a fair, only to find that many of the visitors are not potential buyers. For successful selling in fairs it is essential that not only is the fair for the right market segment, but also that it is for the right level in the distribution structure. So you need to be sure that actual importers are visiting a particular fair, and not just retailers, or, worse still, the general public.

Any participation in trade fairs has to be considered most carefully. They are expensive, require a great deal of time and effort on your part, and give you access to only one particular market place. They are certainly not a sufficient means of contact in a country, but as part of a larger programme of visits to individual importers, they might be helpful. A small handicraft business wanting to develop export markets should not feel unduly concerned if it lacks the resources to participate in trade fairs.

Overseas representation

Some handicraft exporters seek to sell in a particular country by appointing a representative. This could be an individual, or a company. The idea is very logical. It means that the exporter has somebody permanently situated in the target market place, without much expense. Representatives usually work on some kind of commission basis, by which they are paid according to the amount of your products they sell. They would take on resposibility for selling in that market, contacting customers and perhaps also exhibiting at relevant trade fairs. Oxfam Trading has occasionally been approached by exporters who are seeking to appoint a representative. We are not in a position to act as a representative, because we have not established a sales structure to sell to other distributors. We have our own shops and catalogue for selling to the public.

The appointment of a good representative can be an effective export-promotion strategy; a bad one can be disastrous. By delegating the responsibility for selling, the exporter stops making any direct effort in that market. If the representative loses interest in the products, perhaps because other suppliers offer representation, sales may not materialise.

For an exporter who feels able to deal with markets directly, perhaps by visits, possibly supplemented by participation in trade fairs, it would not be attractive to appoint a representative to whom a commission has to be paid on every sale.

Merchandising houses

Buyers, as well as sellers, can appoint representatives. Merchandising houses are companies which search for products and supplies on behalf of overseas buyers. Like a seller's representative, they do not normally make actual purchasing commitments. Instead, they act as a means of introduction between the exporter and customer, and offer an import service. They would usually work with samples, collecting these from exporters, and then displaying them to their customer contacts, either individually or perhaps in specially arranged exhibitions for several customers.

Buyers use merchandising houses in order to avoid expensive and time-consuming overseas tours. Many buyers without experience of travelling to countries which produce handicrafts lack confidence in their ability to locate good suppliers. A company specialising in sourcing products can provide that service, while offering generally more favourable terms of trade, and the possibility of a more direct relationship with the suppliers than is possible by buying from an importer.

The task of the small handicraft business wishing to export is to **identify potential customers** and then decide how best to contact them. As in all aspects of promotion, the criteria for selecting communication methods are: can you afford them, and will they reach your potential customers? For many businesses, indirect contact — by correspondence, a catalogue and samples — is the only realistic short-term plan, with the resources available. In any case, even if a buyer or merchandising house is contacted directly, through a visit or a trade fair, it will still be extremely helpful to prepare sales literature, such as a catalogue. The customer may then refer to this from time to time when considering new product ranges.

4.2   Buying procedures

Importers make buying decisions in different ways. In Oxfam Trading a group of people meets together in a small committee to look at the many samples we have received. Such meetings are organised at certain times of the year, according to the times we need to plan our new product ranges. The people who attend are not only the buyers, but also those responsible for marketing policy and managing our sales outlets. This method of buying by committee is common. Importers

Robert Davis/Oxfam

A product selection meeting at Oxfam Trading. Every importer must consider the sales potential of a product and the record of the supplier before deciding to place an order.

like it because it enables them to compare the offers from all actual and potential suppliers together at the same time. Buyers for large importing businesses are suspicious of making decisions at the point of contact with a supplier. They prefer to see what else is being offered from other countries.

Your chance of receiving an order depends absolutely on having your sample on the buying table when the decisions are made. Importers generally place orders on the basis of samples, rather than photographs, or memory. However, smaller importing businesses may work differently. In the case of a small craft boutique, the owner/buyer will go on a visit overseas, and make buying decisions on the spot. The risk is not large if the quantities ordered are small. Even then, the buyer will probably not be visiting every producer country, and will still need to receive samples from other suppliers, for the purpose of buying after returning home.

The typical export sales procedure of moving from contact to sample to order is a lengthy one. It is often a source of great frustration to exporters that buyers seem to take a long time in making up their minds. It is not that they are indecisive. Rather, it is that they have to plan their product ranges very carefully.

Consider the whole procedure of Oxfam Trading buying for its shops. Each year we set a **buying budget**, which is calculated according to our sales targets, with an adjustment for stock movement. Financial plans have to start from a sales forecast. So, for example, we might wish to sell £10 million worth of handicrafts in the coming year. However, we have a rather high stock both in our warehouse and our shops, and would like to reduce this by £0.5 million. Then our budget might be as shown in Figure 10:

	£
SALES (RETAIL PRICE)	10,000,000
LESS REDUCTION OF STOCK	500,000
OPEN TO BUY (RETAIL PRICE)	9,500,000
- BUYING BUDGET AT FOB PRICES	2,700,000

Fig. 10: *Oxfam Trading buying budget*

We would calculate that we want to spend £2,700,000 in the coming year. As we place orders, we must monitor our expenditure, so that it does not exceed the total. We also monitor sales, so that we could make revisions to our plans if sales were significantly different from those forecast.

Three times a year we undertake a complete review of the **product range** in order to analyse trends and the performance of each individual product. As a result, we decide to discontinue certain products, which are not selling well. Others which are achieving good sales remain in the range, and will be re-ordered at a time determined by when we need to have stock.

The actual number of products in our range will vary slightly over time, but remains fairly consistently in line with growth. We achieve our sales increases both by adding new products to our range, and by selling more of the products we buy. However, we have to control the number of products in the range according to the space available to display them in our shops and to store them in our warehouse. Our capacity to buy new products each year is therefore limited by the amount of old products which we continue to order, and by the overall size of the range.

The analysis of trends will affect the number of products which we want to include in each category of our range. If floorcoverings are selling particularly well, but garden products poorly, then we would probably choose to include more new items of the former than the latter in the coming year. The comparison of Oxfam Trading's retail product range between 1986 and 1990 shown in Figure 11 reveals the trends which we must follow in our buying decisions. An importer would usually formalise such decisions by detailing in the buying budget an open-to-buy figure for each category of products. This is particularly important when there are different buyers for certain categories. One buyer would not appreciate being told that there is no more money to spend because another buyer spent it all on other categories of products. Moreover, it is in the importer's interest to ensure that the money is spent in line with the sales trends analysed.

These are the factors which influence consideration of new samples, at our meetings which are held three times a year. We receive a great many more samples than we can buy. Of those which we do not buy, a proportion will be kept because we like the product, and may want to buy at a later stage, perhaps in the following year. Others we may try to adapt so that they correspond better with market taste.

| | 1986 | | | 1990 | | |
| Product | Total No. of Products | Total Sales £ | Average Sales per Product £ | Total No. of Products | Total Sales £ | Average Sales per Product £ |
	A	B	B ÷ A	A	B	B ÷ A
Candles	22	113,042	5,138	15	287,297	19,153
Food	11	105,663	9,605	30	511,075	17,036
Footwear	6	70,374	11,729	7	150,141	21,449
Flooring	26	71,654	2,755	34	443,523	13,045
Kitchen	45	151,383	3,364	44	336,525	7,648
Decor	105	360,725	3,435	187	1,149,550	6,147
Clothing and accessories	65	124,868	1,921	147	601,177	4,089
Jewellery	9	5,102	566	181	286,244	1,581
Toys and hobbies	19	31,987	1,683	67	281,524	4,202
Garden	15	81,351	5,423	20	157,166	7,858
Stationery	38	212,739	5,598	37	807,355	21,820
Books	8	38,172	4,771	7	57,345	8,192
Campaign items				8	176,355	22,044
Everyday cards and giftwrap	14	58,044	4,146	13	178,591	13,738
Gifts	115	275,264	2,393	238	1,648,610	6,927
Household	94	581,577	6,186	114	1,230,979	10,798
TOTAL	592	2,281,945	3,854	1,149	8,303,457	7,152

Fig. 11: *Oxfam Trading sales trends in shops 1986-90*

The procedure for selecting products for our mail-order catalogues is broadly similar. We hold separate meetings, but undertake the same budgeting exercise and review of past performance and sales trends. The analysis in Figure 12 shows how product groups perform not only in relation to one another but also to the average for the catalogue as a whole. This assists in planning how best to allocate the space in our next catalogue, in order to increase sales.

CATALOGUE		Xmas 1989	Spring 1990	Xmas 1990	Spring 1991
Average sales per product total catalogue		5405	2879	6097	2899
Wallhangings	No. of Products	6	11	11	12
	Average Sales per Product £	9717	2633	4748	2980
Rugs and floor coverings		12	8	7	8
		3558	4945	11751	5241
Furniture		7	8	4	10
		6497	5489	12329	5132
Toys		31	5	19	1
		5000	1164	5754	2336
Musical instruments		6	7	3	8
		8566	3285	7682	1463
Cushion covers		4	7	5	7
		3160	2546	3446	2929
Jewellery: earrings		5	8	9	9
		2531	2733	3869	2502
Jewellery: other		14	14	15	17
		4161	2192	4707	1598
Clothing		26	29	24	27
		5106	3689	8097	4764
Footwear		3	6	7	5
		8471	3665	7458	2945
Kitchen items		31	16	28	9
		4719	1489	4914	1089
Decor: ornaments		11	9	8	8
		7809	4008	5583	1973
Masks		1	1	1	2
		4577	3092	15081	2331
Tablecloths		3	3	3	5
		3825	3589	5826	3453
Bags		18	14	14	10
		6886	2681	5465	2640

Fig. 12: *Oxfam Trading sales trends in catalogue 1989-91*

A small handicraft business should not expect to receive a quick response in the export market. A great deal of patience is required. **You should never assume that an order is likely because samples have been requested**. One workshop in Kenya produced a large quantity of stock of items sampled to us, in the hope of receiving a positive response. Not only were we unable to place an order, but also the majority of the stock was stolen, resulting in a great loss for the workshop. Nor is it realistic to expect to receive a clear explanation of why products were not selected by buyers. Even in Oxfam Trading, where we have a particular interest in keeping our suppliers informed, it is impossible to write back detailed comments on more than 3,000 samples which arrive at our office each year but are not selected. We try to monitor incoming samples each week. Buyers take forward to the four-monthly meetings only products of possible interest, rather than everything which arrives.

Because of the large number of samples which arrive, we have little motivation to remind suppliers who have not sent samples that we want to see some. There is never a shortage of other things to choose from. A number of small handicraft businesses are not good at keeping customers in touch with new products, or even at introducing new products. No importer can continue buying the same product range every year. **The consumers demand change.** Customers who come into Oxfam's shops expect to see a regular supply of new products, otherwise they get bored and go to other shops.

Importers make their buying decisions with regard to their sales pattern during the course of the year. Most businesses are seasonal to some extent. Those market segments of handicrafts which can be categorised as gifts — which is a good number of them — are particularly seasonal. Oxfam Trading achieves two-thirds of its sales in the last one-third of the calendar year, between September and December. This is because consumers buy most gifts at Christmas. Other products are seasonal because of climatic considerations: woollen jumpers will sell only in winter, sandals only in summer. Importers do not want to hold stocks for long periods of time. They cost money by taking up warehouse or shop space and working capital. Hence, importers buy with delivery dates very much in mind, and expect exporters to respect them. These may or may not coincide with favourable times for production. A supplier of lacquer boxes in Thailand was unable to fulfil an order from Oxfam Trading within our requested time because we placed it at the time of the rainy season, when the lacquer would not dry. Tapestry weavers in San

Pedro de Cajas in Peru do little handicraft work in May, because it is the season for harvesting potatoes, the staple crop.

Importers organise their buying procedures according to the structure and characteristics of the market place in which they sell. Often these are not in harmony with the situation which applies in the country of production, and tensions can arise:

EXPORTER'S SITUATION	IMPORTER'S SITUATION
Produces many different categories of handicrafts, perhaps within a single export business.	Market place segmented and specialised, with different companies or buyers.
Supply varies according to availability of raw materials and labour.	Demand varies according to consumer spending habits.
Wants continuity and regularity of orders.	Must constantly search for new products.
Needs information and reactions to samples and sales.	Tends to communicate only about products they are interested in buying.
Likes quick decisions and generous production time.	Makes decisions slowly but tends to expect quick response to requirements.
Likes to encourage creativity.	Often insists on standardisation according to sample.

Effective contact with overseas customers requires exporters to know about their procedures and timetables. It should be one of the points of information to be obtained as soon as possible in a relationship. A small handicraft business needs to be informative to the customer, too. If there is limited production capacity, or seasonal variations, the potential customer should be told this. It is much better to do so at the outset in a relationship than to fail to fulfil an order subsequently because the patterns of supply and demand were not in harmony.

4.3 Contact by correspondence

In all your contacts with a customer, you will be communicating something about your business. If you write letters by hand rather than on a typewriter, or set them out untidily, the recipient might well conclude that you are not very efficient, or insufficiently resourced to be able to fulfil an export order. Poor quality photographs or printed information would imply poor quality products or service. Your promotional literature is your business dress. Dress well, and you will make a favourable impression.

The essence of communication is to give the right information in the right way. A first point to consider is the language to use. It is almost always acceptable to communicate with overseas customers in English, which is the most widely used commercial language in the world. It is often absolutely necessary to use it, because the potential customer would not understand another. If you are able to communicate in the language of the country to which you are writing, this is always better, of course. It gives confidence to the buyer that you are knowledgeable and serious. However, it might not be possible for you to produce sales literature in more than one language. In that case, it is best to use English, unless you are primarily promoting your products to a country or countries where that is not the first language.

A letter of introduction to a potential customer should contain the following information:

- your full name and address;
- the reason why you are writing;
- background information about your business;
- a description of your products and supply capacity;
- the specific purpose of the letter.

Check these against the example opposite.

The information supplied here is **specific** and **relevant**, and the **purpose** of the letter quite clear. It deserves a reply. What should be avoided in letters of introduction are incomplete information, poor grammar, spelling and punctuation, and requests which are too general or unclear.

HANDICRAFT CO-OPERATIVE EXPORT LTD.
(HANDCOOPEX)
P.O.BOX 385
MBABANE
SWAZILAND

Telephone and Fax: 48326   Telex: 2413

Mr. Edward Millard   2nd June 1991
Oxfam Trading
Murdock Road
Bicester
Oxon. OX6 7RF
England.

Dear Mr. Millard,

    We were given your name and address by Mrs. Vera Turnbull of Swazicraft, who
we understand has been supplying Oxfam Trading for some years. We are writing to
enquire whether our recently formed co-operative society could also offer you
products for export.

    HANDCOOPEX was formed last year as a result of a series of meetings among
experienced producers looking for new marketing opportunities. Sales outlets are
limited in our small country. We are seventeen members, 10 men and 7 women,
producing beaded jewellery and sisal baskets. We have a range of 25 products in
all, employing traditional colours and symbols with which I believe you are
familiar. Given our commitments in the domestic market, we are hoping to export up
to 100 jewellery items and 150 baskets per month.

    Because we are new, we have not yet been able to produce a catalogue.
However, I am enclosing two colour photographs to give you an idea of what our
products look like, and also a price list. I do hope you will be sufficiently
interested to request a few samples. We should be happy of course to supply any
further information required.

        In anticipation of your kind reply.

        Yours sincerely,

        Kenneth Mbata,
        President

Fig. 13: *A letter of introduction to an importer*

Try to address people correctly. If you want to write to the Buyer or Managing Director, but do not know who that person is, you should write 'Dear Sir or Madam'. Do not assume that only men have positions of importance in importing businesses. 'Ms' is now the generally accepted way of addressing women. If you know the name of the person, use it, but normally not the person's first name in the early stages of a relationship by correspondence. Also be careful about the name of the country. For example, England is one part of Great Britain, which also includes Scotland, Wales and Northern Ireland. Oxfam Trading sent a letter to a contact in Zimbabwe, just after it had changed its name from Rhodesia. By mistake we put 'Rhodesia' on the envelope. It was returned to us, marked 'Country not known'. The sensitivities of people should always be respected in business relationships.

Oxfam Trading sometimes receives letters from would-be suppliers who do not offer specific products, but rather a willingness to supply whatever we would like. This is not wise. The exporter should make the opening offer with a **clear description of what is available**. Although it is good business practice to invite customers to offer ideas for other products, not to have a definite range on offer destroys the importer's confidence. It is rare for an importer to start developing new ideas with an unknown contact. New product development usually comes along later in a well-established relationship.

It is a good idea to prepare some sales literature to be included in the letter of introduction. What the potential customer wants to know — if there is any interest at all — is definitely more about the products, and possibly a little more about the export business. At the very least, a **price list** should be prepared and printed. This serves two purposes: it provides a list of the products on offer, and should also give details about export arrangements. Handcoopex's price list might look like the example in Figure 14.

Product code numbers assist identification and avoid confusion. A **price list should always bear a date**. Handcoopex's decision to send two photographs is reasonable. The cost is quite small, and they convey much more to a buyer than a list of products alone. Would-be exporters sometimes feel that they need to produce a printed catalogue before they can approach overseas customers. It is not necessary, especially when a few photographs could adequately communicate the important features of the product range. The photographs should be labelled with code numbers which relate to the price list.

HANDICRAFT CO-OPERATIVE EXPORT LTD.
(HANDCOOPEX)
P.O.BOX 385
MBABANE
SWAZILAND

Telephone and Fax: 48326   Telex: 2413

EXPORT PRICE LIST 1991

Product Code No.	Item	Price US$
Beaded Jewellery		
J 1	choker, 1' drop	3.75
J 2	' 2' drop	4.50
J 3	' 3' drop	5.25
J 4	necklace and pendant	4.75
J 5	bracelet .'	2.00
J 6	bracelet, 1'	2.50
J 7	bracelet, 1.'	3.50
J 8	double bracelet	3.50
J 9	earring, 1'	2.00
J10	' 2'	3.00
J11	' 2.'	4.00
J12	Royal Swazi necklace, 3' drop	8.50
J13	Royal Swazi bracelet, 2'	4.50
J14	Royal Swazi earring, 2'	3.50
J15	ankle bracelet	3.50
J16	hair band	1.50
Sisal Baskets		
BS1	round basket 6' diam.	4.25
BS2	' ' 8' '	4.75
BS3	' ' 10' '	5.25
BS4	' ' 12' '	5.75
BS5	tray, 9'	5.50
BS6	nesting s/2 8'h x 8'd and 6'h x 5'd.	8.50
BS7	sweets basket 3' diam.	2.00
BS8	oblong basket 8'	5.50
BS9	oblong basket 10'	6.00

Notes

1. All jewellery items supplied in assorted bead colours unless specified otherwise by customer.
2. Sisal baskets can be supplied only in assorted colours and designs.
3. Earrings are for pierced ears only.
4. Jewellery items are normally packaged individually in polythene bags. Special packaging can be negotiated.

Terms of Trade

1. Prices are FOB Mbabane, packed for export.
2. Payment by letter of credit or against documents through our bankers: Royal Swazi Bank Ltd., P.O.Box 387, Mbabane. Account No/Name: 32681-4 HANDCOOPEX.

Fig. 14: *Export price list*

Fig. 15 *Export catalogue (cover page)*

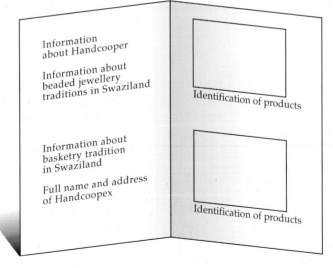

Fig. 16: *Export catalogue (inside pages)*

It should not cost very much to produce a small catalogue of colour photographs, which presents some information about the products, and a little about the exporting business. This would give the impression of good preparation and organisation for export trade. Handcoopex could, for example, produce a single folded piece of paper, laid out something like Figures 15 and 16.

A small handicraft business wanting to export has to decide what it can afford by way of sales literature. If it goes to the expense of producing a small catalogue, it might be reluctant to send it out with an initial contact letter, given that most letters will not receive a response. However, it might make the difference between getting a response and not. It is important to plan beforehand to whom the catalogue is going to be sent. Printed catalogues are a luxury beyond the reach of most small handicraft businesses. The main cost of them is in the process of printing colour transparencies. A black and white printed catalogue can be produced more cheaply, but is rarely very effective in communicating the quality of a product. It is certainly not worthwhile spending most of your promotional budget on printing a catalogue. Some exporters have done so, and found they still have most of them in a cupboard a year later for lack of contacts to whom to send them. Other exporters have made the mistake of obscuring their offer with too much general information. A catalogue is a document in which to promote products with specific information about them, and a clear indication of how to obtain them. Promotional materials are only one component of a promotional strategy for contacting customers. They must not be used as an excuse for not planning a dynamic promotional programme.

Whatever type of catalogue you produce, it is best not to put a date on it, and to keep the price list separate. The prices may need to change, and it is a good idea to print a new one each year bearing the actual date. This gives customers confidence that they have the current information. However, you do not want to have to reproduce the catalogue every year.

As was stated in the example letter, the main objective of a catalogue is to obtain a sample order; and the main objective of seeking an order for samples is to get a bigger order for stock. Samples should be sent to a potential customer only on request. Importers will not welcome receiving samples which they did not ask for, especially if they are required to pay for them. It may well be different with existing customers, who will tend to accept, and perhaps even expect, samples of new products from established suppliers. There is no reason why a new contact who requests samples should not be invoiced for them. As for the cost of sending them, it is a question of judgement. It might create customer goodwill to write off the cost as a promotional expense; conversely the exporter might feel that this would be unjustified. Do make sure to send them by the cheapest means, unless the customer specifies something different. If the package is small and light, air parcel post will usually be a good compromise between speed and cheapness. You should not send sample consignments separately by air freight or sea freight, unless by agreement with your customer. They would normally be very expensive because of the customs and agency costs added to even the smallest consignment. All too often, Oxfam Trading receives small sample packages by air freight, because the exporter did not understand about the costs of export formalities. In countries where the postal service is extremely unreliable, it can be reasonable to send small sample packages by private courier service. These, like parcel post packages, are delivered directly to the customer. Hence, although the cost might seem high, there are no additional importing costs involved.

When sending samples, you should choose items of **average quality**. If you gain an order on the basis of a sample of exceptional quality and then fulfil the order with an inferior quality, the customer will be upset. Keep some kind of **record** of what is sent: a duplicate sample, photograph or description. Remember that it might be a long time before you receive an order. This is why a code number system will help. You can keep a detailed description of each product against each code number. Oxfam Trading received a sample of a painted *papier mâché* box from Kashmir, India. Two years later we ordered stock for our catalogue sales. We sent a photograph, but the film was not a good quality, and the pretty yellow colour of the box appeared green. The exporter could not remember the product, and had not kept a reference or description, and so followed our photograph. We received a beautiful quality box, but in green, whereas our catalogue — which photographed our sample properly — offered to our customers a box in yellow. Several customers returned the green box we sent them, because they had ordered yellow in order to match a particular decorative scheme in their house.

4.4 Meeting buyers

Personal contact with customers is the best way to create mutual understanding, and establish a good relationship. Hence, small handicraft businesses which want to export, or have already started, should **plan to make a visit overseas** if this is at all possible. Much of the success of a trip depends on the **preparation** made beforehand. The itinerary must be planned to take you to where your potential customers are. You cannot visit all the market places, so you must select carefully according to where you have decided to concentrate your promotional effort. Work out how many days you need in order to go everywhere you want to, or can afford to. You must try to use every possible moment constructively. Start planning well in advance so that you can find out about plane and train timetables, and fares. A good local travel agent is an invaluable friend when preparing an overseas visit.

Inexperienced travellers often undergo two shocks. The first is the extent to which the cost of living in countries which import most handicrafts is higher than in those which produce them. A budget which would be sufficient to travel for a month at home might last only a week overseas. It is difficult to find cheap accommodation or restaurants. The second shock is the degree of formality and the limited time available for meetings in many importing businesses. Buyers are used to setting appointments, and to visitors keeping them punctually. While established customers might offer a visitor half a day or a whole day of their time, and perhaps help with travel and accommodation arrangements, new contacts would not normally do this. The culture of the market is one in which the seller has to organise around the buyer's availability. **Appointments should be made in advance**, and **confirmed by telephone** on arrival in the country.

The expectations in this respect are often quite different when an importer makes a visit to an exporter. On very many occasions, I myself have experienced the most generous hospitality from small handicraft businesses to whom I am perhaps making an initial visit. People make themselves available not just to talk for as long as I need, but also to travel with me to see production centres. It is rare that an importer behaves so generously when an exporter makes a visit.

If you do have an opportunity to travel, then take a good quantity of business cards, sales literature and samples. This unfortunately means carrying a lot of weight, but it is essential for you to have examples of your products with you. Like an export catalogue, a sample selection does not have to comprise your whole range, merely a good representation of what you want to sell.

Just as an overseas visit needs preparing for, it also needs **following up** afterwards. You need to send any information or samples requested, and make sure you maintain contact with buyers who showed interest when you visited. For this purpose, keep detailed notes during your meetings. Unfortunately, exporters who make overseas promotional visits are not always as serious as they should be. Some — never the owners of small businesses, but employees who have been given the opportunity of a business trip — treat it as something of a holiday or shopping trip. It is sensible to allow additional time for sight-seeing or shopping in an itinerary, so that the essential business is not neglected, but you can also relax and enjoy the visit as much as possible.

A number of business travellers find it helpful to record information in a formal way on a contact sheet. This helps to ensure that you find out what you need to know, and that you actually do what you need to do when you get back home. See Figure 17, for example.

CUSTOMER CONTACT SHEET

NAME AND ADDRESS ....

....

TELEPHONE   ....

TELEX   ....FAX..

CONTACT NAME   ....

PLACE OF CONTACT ....

BRIEF DESCRIPTION OF COMPANY..

....

MAIN POINTS DISCUSSED..

....

BANK DETAILS   ....

....

PREFERRED PAYMENT TERMS...

FOLLOW-UP REQUIRED...

....

Fig. 17: *Record of a contact made overseas*

A contact sheet would similarly be a useful way of recording meetings that take place at a trade fair. If you are tempted to consider participation in a fair, your criteria for choosing which one should be:

Location: it must take place in the target market place.

Popularity: it must attract the largest number of visitors among your target customer group.

You must attempt to research information about exhibitors and visitors at previous fairs. Not all fairs are well-established or well-attended. New ones regularly appear, but are not necessarily successful. In London in 1989 a first World Handicraft Fair was organised. It was open to both trade buyers and the British public, and was designed to display the full range of handicraft products. Both exhibitors, not wishing to spend a lot of money to participate in a new fair, and buyers, unattracted by yet another fair, stayed away and the event was unsuccessful.

Many fairs are very well-established and attract not only national, but also international buyers. The annual gift fairs at Birmingham and at Frankfurt in Germany in February, and at New York in August are among the most important for handicrafts, and are visited by importers as well as retailers. There is usually a waiting list to get a stand at these fairs because they attract so many important buyers. Another specialist handicraft fair which appears to be establishing itself is the Salon International de l'Artisanat d'Ouagadougou (SIAO), a bi-annual event in Burkina Faso, West Africa, which attracts exhibitors from all over Africa and buyers from inside and outside the continent. This is especially helpful for the development of trade between African countries.

An exporter exhibiting at a trade fair for the first time would not necessarily expect to make a profit on orders obtained. Many buyers would not place orders, but simply take away information or request samples. The follow-up to participation in a fair is what counts. **The real objective is to make contacts**, and then subsequently to convert contacts into contracts.

Although fairs are usually organised according to trade segment, some are set up specially for the promotion of exports from developing countries. In this case handicrafts might find themselves on display alongside industrial products and commodities. Although many visitors would not be target customers, such fairs may attract importers interested in buying from countries which produce handicrafts. There are also examples of trade having started up between countries exhibiting, who were previously unaware of one another's products. The best established of this type of fair is the annual Partners for Progress in Berlin, which has run since 1962.

A number of small handicraft businesses have managed to participate in an international trade fair which they could not normally afford by joining with other exhibitors from their country, and having one stand together. Given that the main costs of participation are not just the stand rental but also the air-fare for the exhibitor and the freight for the samples, the saving in a joint stand is not necessarily very large. It is important not to try to economise on actual participation. It is rarely worthwhile to send samples to a fair unless you can be there in person. Buyers will expect the seller to be available, and you may need to negotiate contracts. Moreover, not to go means missing other opportunities: learning the reactions of visitors to your samples, seeing the products of competitors, and going out after the fair to make visits and study the shops. Joint stands are usually organised through the relevant crafts export promotion department of the exhibiting country's government. Sometimes there is financial assistance available.

A stand at a fair, like a shop, needs to attract visitors by the **quality of its display**. Just as a busy shopper going to the town centre has not time to look in every shop, nor has an importer time to stop at every stand in a fair. The largest fairs attract well over a thousand exhibitors. Buyers will have their eyes on a stand for a few seconds while they walk past. In these few seconds you have to catch their attention. The lay-out of the stand must be carefully planned in advance, both the samples to be offered and the fittings for the stand in which they will be displayed.

It is a good idea to try to arrange a first visit to a country at a time when a trade fair is taking place. If you are planning to go to Europe, January/February would be a good time to choose. Importers are usually still placing orders for the next Christmas season. Getting to know the buying times of your potential customers is an important objective of a first visit.

A trade fair can be a good place at which to make contact with a **representative**, if you are trying to recruit one. Some will have stands, on which they display the products of the different companies whom they currently represent. If you are interested in this approach to selling overseas, it is definitely worthwhile to meet the representative in the market place. That is the only way that you can see what other products are being handled, and get an idea about the person's or company's standing and efficiency. Normally you would look for a representative who deals in similar but not competing products, so that yours may be introduced to the buyers with whom the representative already has contact.

The normal way in which to seek a representative is to place an advertisement in a **trade magazine**. All trades have one or more acknowledged publications in each country which act as channels of communication within the trade. A small handicraft business wanting to appoint a representative to sell toys in Britain might advertise in one of the two recognised magazines. This would also be the place to advertise your products, if you decided to try to attract customers through this means. Advertising would be unlikely to be effective unless there were a representative in the country to whom enquiries could be directed.

Summary

1 There are various ways of establishing and maintaining contact with overseas customers. The best way is undertaking a selling tour. Participation in trade fairs is unlikely to yield satisfactory results except for exporters already established in that market place. An exporter will need some sales literature in order to respond to enquiries, and support promotional initiatives.

2 Importers buy in a systematic way, according to pre-defined budgets and timetables. The exporter needs to understand the procedures of potential and actual customers in order not to miss opportunities for gaining orders.

3 Most contact, at least initially, will be by correspondence. Letters must be well presented and include all relevant information. Exporters need a price list, and preferably some photographs of their products. It is possible to make a useful catalogue cheaply, using colour photographs. Do not print a catalogue until you have a large number of potential customers. If you receive a request for samples, be sure to send average quality, provide the importer with a reference number and description, and record what you have sent.

4 Visits to overseas markets will be expensive and should be planned and followed up carefully. Buyers will expect you to make and keep appointments for specific times. Before participating in a trade fair investigate in detail whether it will give you access to the market place you want. If you are interested in appointing a representative, a fair might be a good place to meet one.

5 SUPPORT FOR HANDICRAFT EXPORTERS

5.1 The international trading environment

International trade is carried out by means of a regulated negotiation between exporter and importer. All traders are subject to the laws of their own country, and to **international agreements** that have been made about trade. Countries make laws about the movement of goods in and out of their countries for three main reasons. First, they can raise revenues, through duties or taxes. Second, their own industries can be protected through restricting imports of competitive products or charging duty on them. These are the two main types of trade barrier. Restriction is controlled by a quota, which allows only a certain quantity of a particular product into a country in any year. Import duty is a charge made on a product when it is brought into the country. Third, the movement of certain products can be prohibited. These can either be things which the government wants to keep in — such as works of great historical importance — or keep out — such as animal products from endangered species.

International agreements have resulted from negotiations among governments at regional, inter-continental and global levels. A number of regional economic organisations exist, such as the European Community, the Association of South East Asian Nations, the Economic Commission of West African States or the Caribbean Community and Common Market. Such bodies are usually characterised by **liberal trading agreements** and **joint investment projects** which enable the member countries to get access to larger markets and supplies of capital.

It is at the inter-continental level that trading agreements affect relations between rich and poor countries. The Lome' Convention was negotiated between the EC and a group of African, Caribbean and Pacific (ACP) countries, numbering 69 in 1990. This trading agreement was first signed in Lome', the capital of Togo, in 1975 and has been renewed in 1980, 1985 and 1990. It established a series of schemes and institutions to further the economic interests of the ACP members in their relationships with EC countries. For example, it permits handicrafts to be exported from ACP to EC countries without restrictions or the levying of import duty.

At a global level, it is the United Nations Organisation (UNO) which regulates world trade. The General Agreement on Tariffs and Trade (GATT) came into existence at a time when trade liberalisation was being favoured, and provided the first structural framework for negotiating concessions in trading agreements for poor countries. In 1963 the United Nations Conference on Trade and Development (UNCTAD) was established. The objective was primarily to create a global forum for international debate and negotiation about changes in the world economic system. It sought to go beyond the practicalities of trade concessions to the philosophy of world trading agreements. GATT's negotiations, like those of the Lome´ Convention, are renegotiated at set intervals, known as rounds. These rounds take place within the negotiating environment established in UNCTAD.

As a result of the creation of UNCTAD and GATT, a new scheme of trading preference for poor countries came into being. The Generalised System of Preferences (GSP) was negotiated in UNCTAD in 1968. It allows most handicrafts to be traded internationally without restriction or the levy of duty. Within GATT, mechanisms were also established to protect the major producers of commodities against fluctuations in world prices. A number of international commodity agreements followed.

This international structure exists to regulate the terms under which countries trade with one another, but **it has not proved as beneficial to poor countries as they had hoped**. Rich countries have not liberalised trade to the extent of allowing imports to threaten their own industries. For example, the Multi-Fibre Arrangement limits entry of textile exports from poor countries to the EC. In the second half of the 1970s and the 1980s there was a tendency towards a re-erection of trade barriers, in order to protect domestic industries in difficulty. In Europe, EC members are committed to the dismantling of individual country barriers by the end of 1992, under the terms of the Single European Act. However, it is not expected that access to European markets will increase overall as a result.

The agreements regarding handicrafts have not generally changed in the periodic re-negotiations of agreements, and are, for most product types, unrestrictive. Oxfam Trading imports under both GSP and the Lome´ Convention. Most products enter without quota restriction or the levy of duty, provided that the exporter supplies correct documentation. The regulations affecting the entry of those products subject to control are often specific to certain countries of origin, and may change from time to time. Details should be checked with the relevant government export office.

The system which is used to administer international trade is a **customs tariff** nomenclature. It is a system of identifying by a number each different type of product, according to the materials used. There are two systems in widespread use, one relating to the EC's Lomé convention, one to UNCTAD/GATT's GSP. There is practically no difference between the provisions of the Lomé Convention and those of GSP as regards handicrafts.

5.2   Trade promotion programmes

Foreign trade has a vital role to play in economic development. Exporting provides the foreign exchange necessary to import essential development requirements such as capital goods and fuel, as well as basic needs for the population. Handicraft export promotion adds value to raw materials available in the country; there is no imported element in most products. Handicraft production provides work for people, often in rural areas, often women. It usually requires little investment. It preserves cultural traditions, and maintains people in their traditional lifestyles. Handicrafts are produced to fulfil local consumption needs, not the need for foreign exchange, and exporting them is a fairly new activity for many countries. This is why inexperience and lack of business expertise is to be found in the sector not only at the level of the small-scale producer, but also within the governmental agencies and other bodies in the producing countries who have the responsibility for promoting export trade. In response to the need to support poor countries in their efforts to trade profitably, GATT set up in 1964 the International Trade Centre (ITC). In 1968 it was put under the joint administration of GATT and UNCTAD, and in 1973 was designated by the Social and Economic Commission of UNO as the focal point in the United Nations system for technical co-operation with poor countries in export promotion.

ITC has an extensive programme to assist the promotion of all types of exports, including handicrafts.[8] It covers every aspect of the trading process:

- The establishment of national trade promotion strategies in conjunction with the government of the country concerned;

- The creation and strengthening of national trade promotion agencies and, through them, the support of Chambers of Commerce and other business organisations;
- Market development through research, the definition of strategies, product development and promotional techniques (ITC carries out these functions in association with all parties in the foreign trade sector, from trade promotion officials to individual exporting firms);
- Advice and contacts to enable exporters to improve their access to information, quality control, packaging, costing and pricing, publicity, financing and other specialised services;
- The production of training materials and the organisation of training courses;
- Research and publications on trade promotion issues, market surveys, business management and other relevant matters. It publishes a quarterly magazine, *International Trade Forum.*

ITC has many representatives assigned to technical co-operation projects inside countries, and these include experts on handicraft promotion. It does not maintain representative offices overseas. The point of contact is through the government of the producing country, in which one person will be responsible for co-ordinating with ITC if a programme is being undertaken. Institutions of UNO work through governments, in response to requests from them. The Resident Representative of the United Nations Development Programme (UNDP), to which ITC is directly responsible for implementing UNDP-financed projects in poor countries, is another point of contact.

ITC claims to have a special interest in **supporting the small-scale sector**: 'Small and medium-size enterprises in developing countries frequently face numerous problems in exporting. For instance, they often lack staff skilled in management and marketing, as they tend to be production-orientated. Export financing may be difficult to obtain because they have little or no experience in overseas marketing. Their limited bargaining power, a result of their small scale of operations, hinders them from obtaining raw materials they need at reasonable prices, whether from local or foreign sources. Their small size and shortage of marketing skills also pose problems in adapting products to foreign demand, controlling quality for export, packaging goods for shipment and conducting research to find sales openings. For the same reasons, they are often not able to handle complex export paperwork and formalities'.[9]

Oxfam Trading has known a number of small handicraft businesses which have benefited from programmes such as participation in a trade fair or a visit to an overseas market, sponsored by ITC. We have regularly met ITC experts engaged in developing handicraft promotion programmes in producing countries. Even where there is not a programme being undertaken, it would normally be worthwhile to make contact with the head office in Geneva to find out about written materials and perhaps past activities in a country.

ITC co-ordinates its activities with many other agencies who have an interest in supporting international trade, for example, the Import Promotion Offices, which are to be found in more than 20 countries which import handicrafts. Handicraft exporters would normally find it worthwhile to make contact with the Import Promotion Office in any country in which they want to sell their products. Contact would certainly be useful if an exporter is visiting a country. They are governmental institutions, established specifically in order to assist the importation of products from certain countries. They deal directly with exporters, as well as with governments of exporting countries, and with ITC. The range of services which they can offer varies. Oxfam Trading is sometimes contacted by Britain's Import Promotion Office with a view to receiving trade missions from a particular country, whose programme the office is organising. ITC maintains a directory of Import Promotion Offices, listing their addresses and the services they offer, updated annually.

Small handicraft businesses are often dubious about contacting organisations of overseas governments or international institutions. Sometimes, it is true, they cannot provide much practical assistance. Yet they are well-resourced to offer services or at least information. As with any requests for assistance, you need to follow three rules: be **specific** in what you ask, be **realistic** in what you hope to get, and do not use the contact as an excuse for not doing all the other things you need to do in order to find out the information your business needs. Remember **it is you who will have to market your products**; nobody else will do it for you.

An example of a fairly straightforward request to make of Import Promotion Offices would be details of trade magazines relevant to your products. These are a valuable source of information and contacts in the country in which they are published. Reading should be a part of any export marketing activity. It is not something to do just once at the initial investigation stage. Ask the Import Promotion Offices about their own publications. Most produce written material on such things as market trends, export-import procedures, and efficient fulfilment of orders. You should also approach the trade promotion agency in your own country. A number of them produce information sheets and booklets on export procedures and services.

For a general range of publications on all aspects of business management, including marketing, it is worth contacting the International Labour Office (ILO). Like ITC, this is a United Nations agency. It is concerned primarily with employment and, as such, supports the promotion of labour-intensive enterprises.

Another organisation which produces a range of publications is the International Chamber of Commerce (ICC). Like those of ITC and ILO, its publications list is a useful resource for selecting titles which seem particularly useful to you. ICC is a grouping of companies and business associations in more than 100 countries. It formulates policy for the business community on such matters as banking, taxation, international investment and trade. It maintains close links with the trade bodies of the UNO and EC, in order to represent the interests of the private sector. ICC Publishing SA is one of its specialist arms.

Other international agencies provide programmes of assistance to the handicraft sector. Within UNO the 1990s have been declared the World Decade for Cultural Development. The United Nations Educational, Scientific and Cultural Organisation (UNESCO) has launched a ten-year Plan of Action 1990-1999 for the Development of Crafts in the World, with the objective of undertaking a 'harmonious, coherent and concerted action to safeguard and develop the cultural, social and economic impact of crafts'.[10] The Plan recognises that support to the crafts sector must be approached with respect to the whole production and promotion process. It also seeks to bring together the efforts and resources of the various international organisations and, within producing countries, different government departments who have an interest in crafts. Part of the planned programmes are concerned with marketing, and will supplement and co-ordinate the work of other institutions of UNO, including UNCTAD and ITC, and of the Import Promotion Offices.

Within the Lome' Convention, the Centre for the Development of Industry (CDI) was founded in 1977 to help to establish and strengthen industrial enterprises in the ACP states. Export marketing assistance has been added more recently to its programmes. Information is available directly from CDI or from the representative — known as an antenna — who has been appointed in each ACP country, within a relevant government department.

The agencies mentioned all have an interest in handicrafts as part of a general brief of trade promotion. A new organisation, based in

London, called Artisan Link Ltd.,which would specialise in craft marketing and assistance, is also being planned, with the support of UNDP and EC. This initiative is in response to an idea promoted by Oxfam Trading.

An exporter must try to keep in touch with programmes which might be organised at any time by one of a number of agencies or institutions. The best point of contact is the government office responsible for handicraft export promotion.

5.3   The alternative trading network

Many of Oxfam Trading's suppliers export to several countries, but only to alternative trading organisations (ATOs). Oxfam Trading is itself an ATO. There are a considerable number of these in the countries which import most handicrafts. What characterises them is their philosophy about international trade. This can be described as follows:[11]

- Working together with the poor and oppressed in the Third World on the basis of justice and solidarity, aiming at the improvement of living conditions, mainly by means of promoting trade in products from these countries.
- Providing information when selling products, in order to make consumers aware of unfair international trade structures.
- Campaigning for fairer trading conditions.
- Reflecting in their own structures a commitment to justice, fair employment, public accountability and progressive working practices.

ATOs bring into public debate issues of international trade which adversely affect poor people, for example, the protectionist policies of rich countries. They signal the consequences of practices in large-scale production, such as land clearing or the use of chemicals, that threaten not only poor people but also the world's ecological balance. They are primarily concerned to show by example that it is possible to trade in a way which is **fairer to small-scale producers**, and more **respectful of the environment**, while still favourable to consumers. They want to take out of the distribution chain, traders who add cost but not value to the products, in order to create as direct a link as possible between producers and consumers. Their objectives go further: to the **mobilisation of consumer pressure** on other retailers to follow trading practices which are more supportive of producers, and which would ultimately empower them to earn more for their production.

ATOs have to work within the realities of the market place. There is no alternative to getting the marketing mix right. What is new about their approach is their promotional method. In the way they conduct trade they offer an alternative to distribution structures dominated by profit-seeking intermediaries. **ATOs bring producers and consumers closer together**. This requires them to address the problems which small-scale producers face, such as lack of knowledge and information, working capital difficulties, inexperience and lack of confidence. ATOs undertake programmes of assistance designed to alleviate these.

For many small-scale handicraft exporters, ATOs would not be potential customers, or sources of support. The type of exporting organisations which ATOs favour are those in which the producers themselves are involved in the management, such as a co-operative, association, union or ATO in the producing country. Almost always acceptable, too, are organisations established by an external agency, either local or foreign, where any profits are destined for the benefit of the producers in some way. Many voluntary agencies and churches establish small handicraft projects, which are not always managed with much participation from the producers, but which offer better than average terms of employment and often social programmes as well. The types of export business with which ATOs are generally cautious about becoming involved are those run by private business people and government agencies. Oxfam Trading sometimes buys from both types of organisations, where there is evidence that they fulfil our criteria, but the majority of approaches we receive are turned down. If you want to contact ATOs as potential customers, then you will need to satisfy them about the ways in which your business **benefits the actual producers**. Unlike conventional importers, ATOs rarely trade with an exporter without visiting at least the business office and often also the production centres.

ATOs concentrate on two types of product ranges: handicrafts and foodstuffs. Some trade mostly in one of these, some in both. More than 90 per cent of Oxfam Trading's sales of imported products are handicrafts. The attempt to sell the whole range of handicraft products is another reason to make ATOs attractive to exporters, who may not need to look for different customers for different parts of their product range. ATOs' interest in handicrafts derives from their importance as a source of employment in the producing countries.

There are several ways in which ATOs support small handicraft businesses:

Use of profits: ATOs do not seek to make large profits, but enough to stay in business. Profits are used for assistance programmes and education and campaigning work. Some ATOs, such as Oxfam Trading, return a dividend to some of their suppliers, which is a percentage of the trading profit.

Prices paid: ATOs try to pay the best price which the market will bear, and which is reasonable in terms of the local situation in the producing community. They might offer a higher price than the exporter is asking, if they are able to do this without prejudicing sales potential.

Provision of working capital: ATOs send advances with orders where this is necessary in order to finance production. This often represents the difference for a small handicraft business between being able to accept an order or not. Local borrowing may be either difficult or expensive or both.

Communication: ATOs see the relationship with a supplier as a partnership in which both are engaged in securing the best arrangement for producers and consumers. They understand the need of exporters to receive information about samples sent, deliveries of stock consignments, and sales achieved, and to maintain a regular dialogue about plans and activities which affect the trading relationship.

ATOs are not a soft option in the market place. They are in competition with other importers, and must have a product which is sufficiently attractive to consumers. Oxfam Trading cannot sell products which are poorly designed, or of bad quality, or too expensive, just because we want to support the exporter. It is better to support the process of improving the product. We are subject to the same pressures as any other retailer. Our customers want to buy their Christmas gifts at the end of the year, and then spend less money in the early part of the year. They want to see new products in our shops and catalogues. We cannot make long-term commitments to handicraft exporters. If sales analysis reveals products are not performing well, we cannot continue to offer them.

What we can do is try to strengthen small handicraft exporting businesses by offering them **services**. These are designed to improve their products and their commercial skills, and to give them the information they need in order to undertake successful promotion to other customers. All businesses need a diversity of customers in order to protect them against the fluctuations in buying levels of each one.

The level and quality of these services vary among ATOs. Oxfam Trading has one of the most extensive programmes, which we make available to our priority trading partners.[12] We work mostly in the following areas:

- product development and design;
- product labels, packaging and pricing;
- technical improvement;
- market promotion;
- export and import procedures, and shipping;
- export market information, including legal requirements;
- business management;
- product costing.

Our services are offered in a number of different ways:

On site discussions with our partners: It is not just buyers and overseas representatives who make visits, but also other departmental specialists, best equipped to address specific issues. For example, the manager of our order and imports office visited Thailand and Indonesia to study the most efficient international shipping routes and banking procedures. Our warehouse manager visited Tanzania in order to advise the governmental handicraft marketing organisation on its warehousing procedures.

Workshops and seminars: For example, book-keeping and financial management workshops have been organised by our office in India on several occasions. An export promotion workshop was held in Colombia, organised in conjunction with the Federation of Artisans of Nariwo and Putumayo.

Consultancies: A British fashion designer went to India to create new products for export markets with one of our suppliers. An industrial designer was engaged to study the production methods and organisational structures of an Indian voluntary organisation for disabled people.

Support of visits by exporters to overseas markets: We assist in arranging programmes and sometimes give small grants to help meet travel expenses of representatives of small handicraft businesses. We collaborate with training institutions in Britain which run business courses, by inviting students to visit and talk with us.

Provision of information, materials, reports and publications: We offer a magazine cutting service, fashion forecasts and market information. We publish our own journal, Bridge News,[13] three times a year.

Assisting in the creation of exporters' sales literature: A small production unit in El Salvador published a single-page colour leaflet, with design and production assistance from our representative. A jewellery exporter in Kenya produced an export catalogue, for which we arranged the colour printing process in Britain.

Collaboration with other agencies: We maintain an active communication with specialist bodies in order to provide advice and information, or simply put partners in touch with other organisations. We maintain a list of the major ATOs in the world and a directory of our partners in producing countries.

Funding: We may fund partly or wholly any of the above activities. Funding may be the limit of our involvement, or, conversely, we may participate in a programme but without granting funding support.[14] Our primary aim is to offer our experience and expertise.

This range of activities has evolved to match the perceived needs of small handicraft businesses. However, it would be quite beyond a single organisation's scope to respond adequately to all the requests it receives. Sometimes exporters make unrealistic demands, based on a misconception of what it is possible to find out without considerable research, or of the actual level of resources and expertise available to an ATO. **Enquiries should always be specific, and limited in range**.

The way forward for improved services to small handicraft businesses is through **co-operation**. In 1988 the European Fair Trade Association (EFTA) was formed by nine ATOs in Europe with the objectives of exchanging information and ideas, and sharing resources in order to make more impact in programmes of support to producers and in education and campaigning work. EFTA members meet in a series of specialist committees. Their programmes, and secretariat, are funded by contributions from individual members. In 1989 a wider network was established in the form of the International Federation for Alternative Trade (IFAT). IFAT membership is open to representatives of producers as well as importers, and is world-wide. Its purpose is to be the main forum for exchange for all organisations engaged in alternative trade. IFAT also operates a membership subscription, but seeks outside funding for special activities. It is the body through which a bi-annual world conference of ATOs is organised.

ATOs as yet represent only a tiny fraction of the world handicraft trade. Moreover, many of those who import handicrafts are small organisations, strong in terms of commitment, but not necessarily in their capacity to sell products and provide services. **They will almost certainly provide a good starting point for export trade because of their more supportive approach**. If an export business fulfils the criteria for ATOs' involvement, then it should try to secure from them the orders, information and services it requires. However, there may well come a stage when the exporter will move on to the conventional market of private business, because that can provide larger orders.

By offering such a large range of products, ATOs are at odds with conventional market segmentation, and as a result are not seen as specialists by consumers. They tend to be weak as a result in selling certain types of products, where they are unable to offer sufficient choice. This is especially true of higher-priced products. Generally speaking, the more expensive a product, the more comparison a consumer wants to make with other products before deciding to buy. The customers of ATOs are often not those with the most spending power, but predominantly younger people who are attracted by the trading philosophy.

The sales performance of any retail business is critically affected by the type of outlets it has: their size, location and standing in the market place. Most ATOs find it impossible to position themselves in their country's market in a way which offers the most appropriate outlets to all of their suppliers. Oxfam Trading is well aware that many of its shops are an ineffective outlet for certain types of product. This is why we have a catalogue as well, and why we try to assist exporters to identify other potential customers.

The degree of engagement with consumers about the purpose of trade varies among different ATOs. The outlets through which they sell partly determine the way of presenting information. In a shop it is difficult to get customers to stop for long to read things. Oxfam Trading therefore concentrates on display cards with very few words. This has the disadvantage of communicating very little! Other ATOs produce much more detailed information sheets about their partners. For all ATOs, the involvement of their customers in their trading philosophy is an integral part of their alternative approach.

Conventional advertising seeks to appeal to the material or emotional well-being of consumers. Typical adjectives used are 'bigger, better, cheaper, satisfying', and typical ideas are that the consumer derives status, beauty, comfort, prestige or admiration from the product. ATOs, by contrast, focus their promotion on the consumer as part of a large human population in a world of finite resources. They expect their customers to be concerned about issues of poverty, injustice, and environmental destruction: the very issues which threaten the producers of the products on sale. Their promotional language is designed to make the consumer feel satisfied by buying in a socially responsible way: the product meets the need not only of the consumer but also of the producer and of the world which we all share. It is a very different approach from that of traditional market economic theory, as expressed in the view: 'Consumption is the sole end and purpose of all production. The interest of the producer ought to be attended to, only so far as it may be necessary for promoting that of the consumer.'[15] Today, there are growing numbers of consumers who believe that these interests should be the same.

In summary, ATOs can be good customers and useful sources of support for the types of small handicraft businesses with whom they work. Their existence might encourage a small business to export when otherwise it might have lacked the confidence to do so. However, if you work with ATOs, you should not expect too much from them, nor overlook your own responsibility in finding out what you need to know for the growth of your business. There are a number of small businesses which, in the hope that some ATO is going to solve all their problems, lapse into inertia.

ATOs are sometimes called 'solidarity organisations'. There exists another type of solidarity marketing structure which belongs to the informal sector. It is really a charity market, in that it depends on the existence of unpaid volunteers to distribute the products. A number of small producers of handicrafts have managed to get their products sold overseas as a result of interested people carrying the products out in a suitcase, storing them in their houses and selling them to friends, or through solidarity groups. Such informal networks are often set up through church organisations. They can provide great support to a production unit, especially by selling at little above the ex works price, but they are obviously very limited in selling capacity.

Summary

1 International trade is regulated by laws and trading agreements. Most trade in handicrafts is free of restrictions, provided that the correct documents are provided.

2 A number of international institutions organise handicraft export promotion programmes. Many countries which import handicrafts have Import Promotion Offices. Therefore, a range of assistance might be available to exporters, who should keep in touch with the government office in their country responsible for handicraft export promotion.

3 Alternative trading organisations (ATOs) in countries importing handicrafts can offer trade on more favourable terms than private importers. They also have a range of services to strengthen small businesses. They confine their support to organisations which promote the interests of producers. If your business fulfils the criteria of ATOs, it might well be worth seeking your export market through them. A federation has been established to link organisations world-wide which undertake alternative trade.

6 DESIGNING AND PRODUCING FOR EXPORT

6.1 Taste in the market place

The marketing process is a circular one, in which comments from actual or potential customers, and sales experience, must be analysed and used to influence future product development. The most difficult stage in export marketing is the early one, in which you have to start with what you already know how to produce, and sound out the reaction in the market place.

Products sell according to their **acceptability** in the market place in which they are being offered. This acceptability is based on their **usefulness** to the consumers, and their **competitiveness** with products serving a similar purpose. Products may be sold either as self-purchases — something for use by the actual buyer, like an item of clothing, or for use in something the buyer owns, like a rug for the house; or they may be sold as gifts — something bought to give to another person. In either case the buyer must recognise a usefulness in the product; it must serve some purpose.

The concept of usefulness should not be confused with that of practicality. Practical means that the value of the product derives from the function it performs, rather than from any other quality the product has. The purpose served by a product may be wholly decorative, for example, a painting or tapestry. It may be emotional, for example, the gift of a heart-shaped box on St. Valentine's Day. The point is not whether the box is big enough to put something in. Its practical qualities are not really relevant. The box serves a different purpose for the buyer; it communicates love to a partner. Most of the handicrafts which Oxfam Trading sells have a value related not primarily to their functional aspect. Why do customers buy from us hand-painted ceramic plant pots, or decorated basketry planters, when a plastic pot is available at a fraction of the price? The answer is that **people value the decorative qualities of our products**.

The usefulness of many imported handicrafts resides primarily in non-practical factors. This is for two reasons. First, most purely practical products are now made industrially, because the industrial process can produce them more cheaply. Where handicrafts have survived to compete with such products, it is only by adopting large-scale, organised and technology-assisted production methods; this is almost exclusively in South-East Asia. Second, consumers are increasingly looking for products which are distinctive by their decorative qualities. Once they have met their needs for practical products, they start to replace or add to these with others which are not only functional, but also beautiful.

These factors have had a profound effect on the role of handicrafts, which are increasingly being pushed away from their main traditional function of responding to practical needs in local markets to that of responding to a taste for distinctive decoration in domestic urban and overseas markets. The process implies a great threat to producers, who no longer know and understand the markets for which they produce. How do rural producers, who have not even visited the capital city in their own country, know what kind of products people will buy in markets overseas? Their lack of knowledge increases their dependence, and hence their vulnerability to exploitation by exporters.

Yet through harnessing the creative talents of artisans, there opens up a path for the future. **It is in the decorative, artistic tradition that the distinctiveness of a country's production lies**. Drawing on this should guide its export design brief. The Makonde woodcarvers of Tanzania and Mozambique should show the world their sculptures, not downgrade their art and abandon their creative skills through the production of ashtrays and elephants. The kantha work embroiderers of Bangladesh should make exquisite bedspreads, cushion covers, or wall hangings, rather than key fobs and greetings cards. No other country can compete with those long-cultivated production skills, nor machines reproduce their beauty. **Countries wanting to export handicrafts should fight off competition from industry by studying their own unique traditions, and adapting these to the life-styles of modern consumers.**

It is the culture of a market place, or the way people live, which determines the types of product they buy. Oxfam Trading was offered highly decorated leather bags from West Africa, with extremely long shoulder straps. When I tried one on, the bag reached the floor. I could not understand why they were made like that, until somebody explained that they were used when riding on camels. As British people do not ride on camels, the product was not useful. We also

Robert Davis/Oxfam

Examples of successful products which have preserved the style of a traditional craft but adapted it to the life-style of the customer.

declined to buy the beautiful *massob* baskets which are an essential part of a house in Ethiopia. This is a round basket which stands table-height, with a lid. Traditional meals are served on the basket, and the family sits round to eat. The product is particular to the culture of the producing country, whereas British people eat in another way.

Similar considerations explain our negative reaction to products which are bought in producing countries by expatriates and the middle classes, but which sell in small numbers now in export markets. Examples are cloth place mats and napkins. Life-styles have changed; people in Britain have less time for washing and ironing. We do not have home helps to do these jobs. More convenient products have come on to the market to respond to our needs: wipe-clean place mats and disposable paper napkins. A misguided search for practical products can lead to design which lessens, rather than enhances, the value of skilful craftwork. For example, very attractive handwoven or embroidered cloth is used to make products such as coin purses or spectacle cases, which people keep out of sight inside a bag, or at home in a drawer; or used to make products like oven gloves or pot holders. Such products are bought almost exclusively for their function, and to make them very decorative adds cost, but not necessarily much value. **Design should seek to derive the highest value from the raw material by using it in the most appropriate way.** A rare animal fibre like alpaca can be promoted as luxurious for its softness and exceptional

92

for its warming properties in an article of clothing. People do not buy clothes just to keep warm, but also to look attractive. Therefore, the decorative qualities of clothes have value. Alpaca fibres have some additional value over wool if used in a rug, but very little in a wallhanging. A sweet-smelling wood loses its additional value if it is made into a box which is then varnished or painted over. Even if it is left natural inside the box, the quality is hidden.

For the most part, consumers overseas associate handicrafts with **natural materials**. The two are in fact unrelated. Handicraft refers only to the means of production, not the materials from which a product is made. Indeed, many handicrafts for sale in domestic markets are made from synthetic materials. Plastic has become an increasingly popular material for sandals and basketry.

The reason why the concepts of natural fibre and manual production process have become related in the consumer's mind is because handicrafts appeal as an alternative to machine-made, mass-produced goods. The same industrial process which mass-produces consumer products creates the synthetic materials used in so many of them. The search for an alternative has focused on products made from the world's natural resources by human labour: on individual, natural creation.

It is generally sound policy when designing for export to avoid using synthetic materials where natural ones may be available at little extra cost. Cotton is appreciated above polyester; silk above nylon; wool above acrylic. Coconut, horn or leather trimmings would invariably be viewed as superior to plastic imitations. In Ecuador, buttons are produced from tagua nut, which comes from the fruit of a tropical palm. Its cultivation provides the local people with an economic alternative to clearing land for agriculture.

There is, in many markets, a growing realisation that the world's resources are finite, and that some raw materials are not easily renewable. Over the past few years, Oxfam Trading's customers have started to question us about why we sell hardwood products, for example. Wood is, of course, a renewable resource, but hardwoods take decades to mature. In most countries, reforestation programmes have not kept pace with tree-cutting, and this has serious environmental implications. The issue is a difficult one, given that so many artisans depend on wood for their livelihood. It is not usually handicraft manufacture which has depleted wood resources. We have taken the view that we should continue to import wooden handicrafts, provided that there is evidence of replanting programmes. We decided to discontinue importation of ebony wood products from Malawi because it was clear that the disappearance of ebony trees was directly linked with handicraft production in that country.

Exporters should be aware that overseas buyers are going to ask questions about the **raw materials** used in the products offered. There has been too much short-term profit seeking in the handicraft trade at the expense of a production community's future. It takes pressure from the market place by concerned consumers to put a brake on the process. Changes in buying habits are coming too late to undo most of the damage done, too little as yet to make a significant impact. The issues, though, will gather support. In handicraft creation, as in all development processes, we should be seeking **sustainable product design**, employing materials whose supply in the future is secure, as far as can be foreseen, and will not have damaging environmental consequences. It is not only wood which causes concern; coral is an example of a resource of the ocean which takes centuries to grow, and which is gathered for handicraft production. It is the exporters, rather than the producers, who have to take the lead on these issues. The vast majority of producers live in such poverty that they cannot afford the luxury of thinking beyond immediate survival.

By the same token, some animal products are not favourably regarded in overseas markets. Trade in ivory was prohibited by international law in 1990. Other products may be legally exported from a producing country but are not allowed to be imported into others. For example, Britain does not allow jewellery made from ostrich egg shells to enter the country, although Botswana exports it. As well as the legal regulations, it is the antipathy of consumers towards the exploitation of animals for financial gain which removes demand. Skins and shells are generally not appreciated, unless they are by-products of animals which are killed for their food value. Crocodiles and snakes, for example, are hunted only for their skins.

The growing concern for the preservation of the world's resources and the avoidance of exploitation of animals is influencing buying habits in the markets of the countries which buy most handicrafts. Consumers are beginning to consider when they buy a product not just the advantages for themselves, but also the effects on the world's ecological balance of producing and packaging it. We are probably at the beginning of a **fundamental change in consumer behaviour**. It is already affecting product presentation and promotion, and, more slowly, production methods. In recent years, there has been a surge of demand for products such as cosmetics which are not tested on animals, organic foods, and recycled paper. A retailer which has grown rapidly by responding to these demands is The Body Shop. It makes

Robert Davis/Oxfam

A basket made from recycled newspaper will appeal to environmentally-aware customers.

products for hair and skin care, free of chemicals, modestly packaged in re-usable bottles.

Recycling is a phenomenon which has always been present in quite a lot of handicraft production. There is now a better opportunity than ever to seek export markets with products made from recycled raw materials. Oxfam Trading sells, for example, rugs from India woven from scraps of material, jewellery from Ethiopia made from melted down old coins, and shirts from Zaire made from flour bags. In Haiti brightly coloured wall decorations made of flattened-out oil drums are exported. In South Africa, stunning traditional designs are reproduced in baskets made of different-coloured plastic coated copper wire. These also find export markets, challenging the preference for natural fibres by appealing to the new interest in recycling.

Exporters should seek every opportunity to promote any aspect of recycling in the products they are selling. If metal, or glass, or cloth is being re-used after originally being produced for something else, it is worthwhile to tell the customer, who will be interested to know that the product consumes less new material. There is sometimes scope to design products out of waste material from other production. An Indian manufacturer of leather sandals made key rings out of leather scraps and sold them quite successfully. Exporters must also inform themselves about all aspects of the procurement of the raw material.

For example, if it is wood, is there a reforestation programme in the area it came from? If it is leather, how are the hides obtained and what is the tanning method?

6.2   Product development

The product range is the most important asset of a small handicraft business. It is what creates the orders which keep it going. What a business must not do is manage its product range as it would a fixed asset — once acquired, forget about it for a while. The product range must never be forgotten about. There is a constant need to **revitalise** it, bringing out new products, and discontinuing others. This may be for a number of reasons, most of which will apply to every business:

- to offer customers something new;
- to replace products which are not selling well;
- to build on the success of products which are selling well;
- to start a new production activity;
- to differentiate your products from those of competitors;
- to offset seasonality in sales;
- to make more profit.

Most products have a **life cycle**, consisting of five stages, as shown in Figure 18.

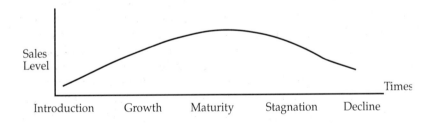

Fig.18: *Product life cycle*

Products vary greatly in the speed with which they pass through the cycle. For exporters and importers alike, the most favourable path is a slow one, with a long flat period of maturity, which enables accurate sales forecasting and reduces the pressure for new product development. But almost every product must eventually stagnate and

96

decline, however successful it is in its peak sales period. This is because **markets are not static**. Tastes change, and this affects a product's usefulness. Products categorised as fashion are usually susceptible to a short life cycle, because fashion trends change from year to year. For example, clothing has been made very loose-fitting in Europe in recent years. T-shirts, jumpers and trousers have been cut wide. At some point, the fashion will change again. When it does, very few people will buy the same shapes of clothes. Exporters will need to renew their product range with the newly fashionable shapes.

Even where taste changes slowly, consumers simply want to see something new each year. Importers must be able to offer new products into the retail market. **Newness is a very important promotional tool**. It is used by advertisers to persuade consumers to buy products they perhaps do not even need, by convincing them that their old products are no longer useful or fashionable or as attractive as those of their neighbours. This is often not true, but people like to buy new clothes, or jewellery, or things for their home or for their friends. Your competitors will be alive to the taste in overseas markets for newness. To keep your customers, you, too, must offer them something new.

It is not just to replace products in decline that a business must keep product development permanently on its agenda. It is to respond to its successes, too. If sales of certain types of products increase, there may well be scope to add new similar items. Perhaps you have responded to a fashion trend, or a development in people's life-styles. Maybe a competitor has disappeared from the market place. If you plan business growth through product development, you would probably build on the basis of what you are selling successfully at present.

Sometimes a business will reach a stage in its development when it wants to begin selling a completely **new range of products**. One reason might be the opportunity to provide work for a new group of people; several of Oxfam Trading's ATO suppliers regularly form new relationships with producer groups and introduce their products to overseas markets. Another might be to reduce dependence on the existing range, which might be quite small or specialist or not selling very well. We have known producer groups discontinue handicraft production altogether and retrain for a different activity.

Another reason might be to combat seasonality. An Indian manufacturer of leather sandals faced the problem of seasonal demand. All his customers were in Europe, where sandals are worn only in the few hot summer months. He adopted a market development strategy at first, approaching importers in Australia and New Zealand, where summer is at the time of the European winter. This balanced demand somewhat but not sufficiently. So he started to manufacture leather bags, and successfully developed a completely new range of these, using machines for stitching.

Most handicrafts employ some materials which have to be purchased. Almost all production units experience problems of rising material costs. Perhaps unwilling or unable to increase selling prices at the risk of losing orders, their production becomes increasingly less profitable. This situation requires a solution which does not harm the producers, as would a reduction in the labour cost of the product. A design change can sometimes provide it. If you can preserve the essential features of a product and thereby maintain your selling price, while reducing the production cost and maintaining the quality, you will make more profit.

Clearly, product development may be inspired by a variety of motives. The form it takes will depend on the needs and interests of the individual business. The basis for approaching it should be a regular analysis of sales trends, production costs and market possibilities. By studying the messages coming from the markets in which it sells, and by thinking about the raw materials and production skills available, a business can guide its product development along a path which is most likely to be profitable. There are other sources of information. Be alert to signs, attitudes, trends that can be read about in magazines, or observed in shops. Existing customers are a key resource for new ideas. Helpful ones — but there are not many of them — will explain why a product has not sold, or a sample was not selected. Sometimes they will make their own suggestions or requests, either for new products or for modest alterations to existing ones. Product development is also concerned with the **adaptation of designs**, in order to respond to requirements in a different market place. For example, Oxfam Trading has to assist suppliers with information about correct sizing in many types of products, such as the right size of hole in a candle-holder. A common problem which we encounter is that wallets are not the right size for British money. We nowadays need wallets which also have compartments for credit cards, which are increasingly replacing cash as a medium of exchange. The sort of wallet we want to buy is traditional on the outside, according to the materials and manual skills available to the producers, but designed inside for the modern British consumer. In the same way, footwear and clothing must be adapted to the size of people in the country to which they are being offered. It is not difficult to get the information about standard measurements of shoe length and width, or of chest, garment and sleeve length in clothing, and the range of sizes usually offered. It is the type of information which an Import

Promotion Office should provide. Oxfam Trading successfully sells hand-knitted jumpers made from handspun alpaca in Peru. The women producers required careful training to get the sizes right for Britain, as British people are larger than Peruvians. Then they had to learn a new set of dimensions when they secured an export order from Japan!

Oxfam Trading's experience is that the majority of small handicraft businesses are insufficiently active in product development. Too often it is we ourselves who have to take the initiative in reminding suppliers of the need to change the product in order to have something different to offer to our customers. We regularly make suggestions for alterations to samples we receive. We do this because we are committed to supporting our priority suppliers. Most importers would happily switch to a competitor if an equally good product is offered. In South America, I visited a production unit from which we had bought clothing twelve years earlier when those designs were fashionable. The same products were on offer again, and indeed the whole product range was the same. The designs had begun to come back into fashion, but in the meantime, the unit had experienced many years of low demand. One way in which exporters could obtain ideas for product development would be to request from customers or Import Promotion Offices copies of magazines which might illustrate the types of product currently being sold in the target market place.

Design and product development are most successful when they **involve the actual producers**. If the people who make the products do not understand what they are to be used for, it is not possible to engage their creative energy in the activity. Oxfam Trading developed some place mats, adapted from traditional floor mats, through our ATO supplier in Bangladesh. When we visited the production centre, in a rural area, the women expressed surprise at our request for 10" and 12" diameter mats, because 'they seem very small to us for sitting on'. Our supplier had not explained to them the idea of table mats. We visited a tribal area in northern Kenya soon after a project had been introduced by an external agency to weave baskets from the local palm leaf. The women producers could not understand how some baskets were being designed so large. Nobody could carry those on their head, full of grain, which for them was the function of a basket. When it was explained that they were in fact laundry baskets, they burst out laughing. Although they themselves did not wear clothes beyond modesty covers, they knew other people did. But the idea of having more than one set of clothes and of making something to keep the dirty ones in rather than washing them straight away was quite bizarre to them.

External agencies who become involved in handicraft projects to try to generate income in poor communities have a special responsibility for design and product development. Producers get very confused and disappointed if they are taught a new design by somebody from outside, but then do not receive orders for it. Yet this often happens. In a project in Central America, I found a warehouse filled with a stock of basketry, which had been financed by an outside agency in the hope of securing export orders. There was a need for a proper analysis of the range and for a programme of product development based on an appraisal of taste and competition in the target markets. Instead, the agency was planning to withdraw from the group because there was no further funding for the project. It is not that starting up new production projects is necessarily wrong; but if it is done, the agency must research the market, involve the producers in creating the product range, and evaluate its performance during the period of commitment.

Export design should emphasise the **distinctiveness of the product**, adapting and promoting it to be useful to consumers in the importing country and responsive to their life styles and concerns. It must also consider the practicality of the product being shipped across the world, and being roughly handled. While good packing should reduce the possibility of breakage, sensible product design can also help. For example, Oxfam Trading imported elephants made of soapstone from India. The trunks broke regularly because they protruded upwards from the body. By re-designing them to go downwards and connect to the body of the elephant, the exporter greatly strengthened the product, and secured a further order which we would otherwise not have been able to give. We did not order a wooden carving from Africa, depicting a woman carrying a basket. We liked the product and its price was competitive. Unfortunately, the wood had been cut so narrowly at the point where the basket joined to the head that it broke. The solution lay in re-designing that section to make it wider, and hence stronger.

It can often be helpful when designing for export to **reduce the size of products which are potentially fragile**. If a decorated ceramic vase can be made smaller without changing its shape or form of decoration, it will retain the qualities which the importer will value, even if it loses its functional use. Importers are likely to feel more positive towards fragile products which are quite cheap, because the loss is not so great if they break.

Cost-effectiveness is clearly a fundamental consideration of exporting. It makes sense to get the most value into the space available.

For this reason, baskets are often offered in nesting sets. The disadvantage with sets is that the importer is obliged to buy an equal quantity of the different sizes of basket, but they may not in fact sell evenly. Oxfam Trading prefers baskets which are narrower at the base than the top, so that baskets of the same size fit inside one another, for economic shipment.

6.3   Quality control

Oxfam Trading once had to discontinue selling a palm leaf shopping basket from India because the handles had not been attached sufficiently strongly to the sides. When the bag was full of shopping, the handles could not support the weight, and broke. This was a problem of quality control. The solution was to extend the handle right round the basket.

A number of problems of unsatisfactory quality relate to the design stage of the product. The first point to be checked is the material used. For example, wood must be properly seasoned. If a product is manufactured when the wood is still wet, it will dry out afterwards, and may crack. This has often happened to wooden products which we have looked at in our selection meetings perhaps four to six months after they were made. It does not give us confidence to place an order. If an item will require frequent washing, such as clothing or bedding, we test the sample. We sometimes find that the cloth has not been pre-shrunk. Dyes are another area of difficulty. If colours are not fast, they will not generally be acceptable. Consumers in countries which import most handicrafts are not prepared to wash items separately by hand.

A group of Indian exporters on a training course for export marketing were shown a beautifully carved wooden box which had been rejected by an importer although the price was competitive. Asked why they thought this was, nobody looked at the hinges inside, which were of poor quality metal, applied with nails. When this was pointed out as the reason, several of the trainees questioned it, asking why it mattered, as you did not buy a box for the quality of its hinges. Quality is a variable concept. Everyone wants products to be of satisfactory quality, but 'satisfactory' means different things to different people. **The quality standards in each market place will be different.** In Britain, as in many other countries, we would insist that it does matter that the quality of the hinges of a box are consistent with the quality of the box itself. We look closely at the details. If you stand in a shop and watch consumers buy products, you will see that they do, too. Any product which opens, like a box or a bag, is immediately inspected inside. Zips are tested for easy running. People want fittings and fastenings to look attractive, and to function properly. Linings and zips should be in a colour which matches the colour of the product. Painted items should be finished neatly, avoiding splashing. Remember that **the whole product will be inspected by the buyer**. Lack of attention to detail will imply lack of understanding of the overseas market's perception of quality, and also lack of control in the production process.

This is an area of considerable difficulty for many countries. The problem may not be a lack of understanding, but a lack of materials of the right quality. Sometimes there is no alternative to importing a component, such as a buckle, zip, or clasp. A more imaginative solution can sometimes be found. A leather-bag manufacturer in Niger commissioned silversmiths to make fastenings for bags, using old jewellery designs. The result was to create a product which did not look like a poor imitation of the industrial process, but a celebration of the artisan tradition.

There must be no compromise on quality when designing for export. As a general rule, it is bad policy to reduce quality in order to reduce cost. If a necklace doesn't close satisfactorily, or the thread breaks, you will not secure export orders, or, if you do, you will not get further ones. Even if it costs an additional 5 per cent to put on the best quality fittings, it will be worthwhile.

The manufacturing process must also be checked for quality. Oxfam Trading declined to buy some cushion covers because the stitching was so poorly finished that the appearance was unsatisfactory. The probable reason was an attempt to keep the price to its lowest possible level. We sent an order for wooden stationery racks only when the manufacturer agreed to cover the nails with a filler, so that when varnished, the fixing could not be seen.

Control of quality must of course be applied strictly in the actual production of an order. Disagreements often arise when an importer claims that the production is not as good a quality as the sample against which the order was made. This is why it is a good idea to **keep an exact duplicate of samples** which are sent to importers. Not only can the actual production be measured before shipment against that sample, but also any complaints will be easier to discuss.

The same standards which apply in the creation of the original design must be followed through rigorously in the production process. The quality of the materials must be consistent. Wood can cause particular difficulties. Oxfam Trading received complaints from customers who bought wooden furniture which had been made using the soft sapwood as well as the hard interior wood. The two were a different colour, and the inconsistency in a prominent part of a furniture piece, such as a table top or bedhead, is not appreciated. An item of clothing was returned to us by a mail-order customer because the manufacturer's name appeared near the hem. It was the end piece of the roll and should not have been used. A jacket was returned because the sleeves and body had been made from different bales of cloth, and did not exactly match. A manufacturer of stoneware accepted an order for candleholders in pairs. When they were packed, the different shades of stone were not matched. The whole consignment had to be repacked in our warehouse, but even then we could not create an exact number of matching sets.

Many handicrafts are made in small-scale workshops, and many orders fulfilled by a large number of different producers. In this situation, the scope for deviation from the norm of the sample is considerable. In order to avoid it, exporters must ensure that **all the producers understand the quality which is required**, and are prepared to make that quality for the price they are being paid and within the time they are being allowed. There have been many examples of quality problems due to lack of understanding of the importance of details. Shape and size are common errors. If an importer orders round baskets, 10″ diameter, that is what should be supplied. If some are sent of a different shape or size, it might not be acceptable to a customer, even if the product supplied is apparently better value. For example, a 12″ diameter basket might be quite unsuitable, if the importer was going to supply to a restaurant, where the size of tables required nothing larger than 10″.

Colour can also cause difficulty. Producers would not necessarily understand why a basket should for example be completely plain, and not use some dyed pieces, for variation. They would not know what the sample against which the importer had ordered was actually like, unless the exporter showed them. Yet probably the completely plain colour is an important detail of the order, and variation is not permitted by the importer. Oxfam Trading often has problems with colour on products which we sell through our mail-order catalogue. Our customers see in the catalogue only the colour of the sample we photograph, and place their order on the basis of that. They expect to receive an identical product. If the colour of the product actually supplied is different, they may return it, and request a refund of their money.

The price paid to the producers will generally have an impact upon the quality of production. Some exporters have introduced systems of bonus payments for work of exceptionally good quality. Conversely, an unscrupulous trader who pays very low piece-rate prices is liable to receive low-quality production. The producers will have to rush their work in order to make the largest number of products in the shortest possible time. Shortfall in quality may also occur if insufficient time is allowed for production. Oxfam Trading received from Africa a consignment of basketware in which many pieces were too small. It was not that the exporter had misunderstood the dimensions required. Rather, the order was too large to complete in the time available, and, not wanting to delay despatch, the production process was speeded up, with disastrous consequences.

Exporters must ensure that producers not only understand the quality requirement but have the financial and technical capacity to adhere to it. They must not buy materials of an inferior quality, for lack of cash, or hurry the order at the risk of poor quality production in the hope of delivering and getting paid earlier. A lot of problems of this nature occur because a contract is not properly discussed at the time of placing it; or perhaps because the producers do not explain their difficulties, for fear of losing the order. The tools required to control quality are usually minimal and simple. A tape measure or measuring rod is often the only one. Basketmakers can make precisely nesting sets of baskets with a simple stick which ensures consistency in the diameters and heights.

The **working conditions** must be favourable for good quality production. Products made in houses can be more subject to soiling than those made in workshop conditions. If this is a risk, an alternative way of organising production needs to be sought. Certain raw materials may require fumigation or similar treatment. This usually needs to take place at the production centre as soon as possible. There can be a period of danger between production and shipment. Consider, for example, this letter received by Oxfam Trading from a supplier in Thailand:

> 'With regards the actual baskets. We are having problems with both insects and mould, especially during this wet season. We can only go to villages, say, once a month and so by the time a finished basket arrives here, the problems have begun. Of course, the villagers find it difficult to understand how a very few minute pin-size holes make the product unsaleable and I expect most of your discerning customers have no concept of the difficulties of a remote hill tribe in the monsoon! We are doing our best to get you the best quality products without it costing us a fortune for rejects – or the villagers

losing out on rejected work. Dry season production is a lot easier and we will try to work for a better system. However, if it is acceptable to you to have part shipments sent, it will lessen the danger of deteriorating products if we can get what we have off to you quickly in reasonable quantities. Part-shipments do, we understand, cost you more but we lose out if we have large wastage due to storage problems in a tropical climate. The alternative is for us to build 'Wastage' into our price and they will cost more! One cannot win.'[16]

Insect holes might not always be visible at the time of production, or even packing for shipment, but the insects might nevertheless be present. So might moth eggs in woollen products. Our supplier in Peru has the opposite problem from the one in Thailand. The production centres for alpaca jumpers and tapestries are high in the mountains, and hence too cold for moths. These can get into the jumpers when they arrive in the capital, Lima, for despatch.

The process of quality control must finally ensure that products are actually ready for packing. We received a consignment of painted lacquerware from Thailand, in which the products had been packed before the lacquer had dried properly. During transit, they stuck to the paper in which they had been packed. Most plant fibres attract mould if not dried out properly before despatch.

The control of quality entails four activities:

Training: to ensure that everybody understands what is involved in producing for export;

Consultation: so that the producers can bring up any difficulties with particular orders;

Organisational control: by which whatever systems are being employed are effectively carried out;

Inspection: to take place before packing.

If producers are adequately trained, consulted and remunerated, they will usually produce good quality. Artisans take pride in their work. A group of painters in Colombia decided to introduce a system of quality inspection within the group. Quality improved as each member sought the praise of a fellow artist. Like anybody else, what artisans resent is unreasonable treatment. Unfortunately, this is what they often receive from exporters whose sole focus in an export contract is the difference between their buying and selling prices.

Quality control means making the product according to the customer's requirement, and to a standard of manufacture which will give satisfaction in use. **The quality of a product is usually remembered long after the price paid has been forgotten.** It is more complicated to implement detailed control systems in manual methods of production than in mechanised ones, and, for the same reason, more necessary. The individual, manual nature of handicraft production is not an excuse for significant variations in quality when fulfilling an order.

The question of quality control is not just left to exporters. There are also laws governing the quality of products which are traded internationally. These apply in both exporting and importing countries. Exporting countries sometimes require quality inspection to ensure that the products being exported are described correctly. Unscrupulous exporters may try to make a false claim about the materials used, with the intention of charging a higher price than the products are worth. Some countries have a label which is attached to the product to confirm that it has passed any required quality inspection. Normally, a document or a stamp is the method of certification. Unlike customs inspection of export consignments, which is a universal practice, quality inspection is not; it applies only to certain products in particular countries. Exporters should find out if there is any such procedure for their products.

Laws regarding importation of products are applied in order to ensure that products entering a country are subject to the same quality standards as apply to those manufactured inside the country. Individual countries have their own laws. In Britain a body called the British Standards Institution prepares national standards for different types of products. Gradually, countries of the European Community are harmonising their laws by introducing common standards. What concerns governments is the **safety** of products. Under the Consumer Protection Act in Britain, all products must be safe for their purpose. For example, children's clothing may not use any form of drawstring around the neck, in case a child should strangle itself by accident. Oxfam Trading has had difficulties under this Act. We discovered that brooches from South America depicting local figures in national dress were made by sticking the head on to a pin which ran through the body. The head was quite easily removed — and hence could have fallen off — leaving a sharp pin exposed. The product was deemed unsafe, and the entire consignment had to be destroyed.

Particular attention is given to the materials used in manufacture. There is a range of laws governing materials which may be used in certain types of products. These laws are particularly strict for products which come into contact with food, and also with regard to toys. It is reasonably assumed that young children may put toys into their mouths. Hence, materials harmful to health, such as lead, may not be employed in products to be used for serving or storing food, or in toys. Exporters wanting to sell painted toys, for example, must find a source of paint which is lead-free. Some products are legally required to carry labels indicating that they comply with safety standards. In 1990 the first standard label common to all EC countries was introduced. This is the CE mark for toys. Any toy exported into any EC member country must carry this label. There are a number of labelling requirements on clothing items. It is an important part of an exporter's research to ascertain precisely what the laws are regarding safety standards of imported products in any countries targeted for promotion.

The responsibility for compliance with legal standards rests with the importer. It is the company which brings the product into the country which must satisfy any enquiry or complaint.

These may come not only from consumers, but also inspectors, employed by governments, who go into shops, and look through mail-order catalogues and other advertisements. Oxfam Trading spends a considerable amount of money each year sending products away for laboratory analysis before placing an order. This expense might not be necessary if the exporter could provide precise technical information about the materials used in the product.

Summary

1 A product's usefulness may derive from its decoration as well as its practicality. Many handicrafts sell because their decorative qualities have value. A country may achieve distinctiveness in its handicrafts by designing with reference to its traditions. Yet a product must always be adapted to the taste of the consumers in the market place to which it is being offered, by being responsive to their life-styles and concerns. Design must take account of sustainability, employing renewable materials, and recycled ones where possible. A fundamental change is beginning to take place in consumer behaviour, in which interest in the environmental consequences of production is as important as the usefulness or beauty of the product.

2 Products are subject to a life cycle, so that sales of an item will eventually decline. For this reason, a business must regularly develop new products. Consumers demand them, and competitors will be trying to meet that demand if you do not. Sales experience, and a study of market opportunities, are the keys to successful product development. Products must always be adapted to the requirements for selling in the target market place, regarding such matters as product size, and efficiency of transportation.

3 Quality control needs to be applied rigorously at all stages of the production and distribution process, starting with the raw materials. Colours should be consistent, and materials properly prepared. Difficulties sometimes result from misunderstanding between an exporter and importer about the level of quality required. There are some strict laws controlling the quality of imported goods. An exporter needs to know about these. Effective quality control requires training and consultation with the producers, and a system of inspection.

7 PRESENTING YOUR PRODUCT

7.1 Labels and packaging

The preparation of the offer to importers needs to follow through from the design and production stages to consideration of the product's **presentation**. There are two possible additions to the actual product: a **label** and **packaging**. To some extent these serve a similar purpose, which may be one or all of the following:

- to guarantee to the consumer that the product complies with legal safety standards;
- to give information about the product;
- to give advice about use or care of the product;
- to make the product attractive to the customer;
- to incorporate the customer's brand name;
- to identify the product to the customer.

Packaging can serve two further functions:

- to protect the product during distribution;
- to make handling and retail display easier.

Packaging is a part of the presentation of a product, and stays with it throughout the distribution chain. It is not to be confused with **packing**, which is the material you add to a consignment for safe transportation as far as your customer. Almost every product can benefit from at least one of the advantages which labels and packaging bring. This is why so many products on sale in the countries which buy most handicrafts have one or the other or both. Manufacturers like labels and packaging because they can be used to promote a brand name; retailers because they advertise the product, make it more desirable, and inform the customer about it. Consumers like them because they provide information and a more attractive product. The government likes them because manufacturers are being honest with consumers about the product. We live in an age of packaging, which most handicraft exporters have been very slow to recognise. Poor presentation of handicrafts reinforces the prejudice that the product may be technologically inferior, and removes demand in domestic as well as export markets.

Most handicrafts benefit from **information** being given about them. The people who make them, the materials and techniques used, can all be of interest to importers and consumers. An exporter can write this information in a letter, but who reads that? Perhaps the buyer, and nobody else. Certainly not the importer's customers. Perhaps they will if they buy from a mail-order catalogue, where the information has been reproduced; but by the time they receive the product, they will have forgotten most or all of that. The point of labels and packaging is that they stay with the product at least until the moment that the consumer buys it, and very often beyond that. In Oxfam Trading we try to inform all the staff and volunteers who work in our shops about the products we sell. We know that the information is not received or read by everybody, and anyway has to be very brief. A lot of our customers ask for information in our shops about the products we sell, and the producers of them. We would be able to give a better service to the customers, and represent the producers we work with much more positively to them, if the information they required was available on labels and packaging.

The first kind of information to which an exporter must give attention is that required by law. Even if no other presentational material is used, any labels necessary to confirm **compliance with legal standards** must be added to the product or to its package. There may be different ways of doing this. Cloth labels which are sewn to the actual product may be required, so that the label remains throughout the product's life. An adhesive label attached to the product or its package may be acceptable. The use of such a label does not imply that the product cannot or should not carry other information, although it is usually most practical to put the legally required information on a separate label.

Next in importance is information regarding the **care of the product**. Any product which requires cleaning should advise its user how best to do this. This applies to all textile products, but also to others, such as wooden kitchenware products. Importers need to protect themselves against complaints by consumers who mistreat products. For example, if a handknitted mohair sweater should be dry cleaned, it would probably not survive very well being washed in a machine. If a consumer did this, a complaint would have much more force if the sweater gave no instructions about cleaning. If a label inside the product said 'dry clean only', the consumer could not reasonably complain.

International symbols for textile care have been introduced. The International Textile Centre Labelling Code consists of five basic symbols. They refer to washing, drying, cleaning, bleaching and ironing, as follows:

Washing

For washing by hand or machine. A number inside the symbol shows the maximum temperature at which the garment should be washed.

Handwash only.

Do not machine or handwash.

Drying

Can be tumble dried.

Do not tumble dry.

Hang dry.

Dry flat.

Cleaning

Dry clean only. A letter inside the circle indicates which solvent should be used.

Do not dry clean.

Ironing

Can be ironed. A line inside the symbol indicates cool iron, two lines warm iron, three lines hot iron.

Do not iron.

Bleaching

 Can use household bleach.

 Do not bleach.

It is often possible to buy cloth labels already printed with these symbols. If labels suitable for your product are already available, it will remove the need to have your own printed. It is equally possible to present the information in words rather than symbols. The important thing is to tell the consumer how to treat the product properly. Textile care labels need to be sewn to the product.

It is important to add a label where a product may not fulfil a customer's expectation. For example, Oxfam Trading sold soapstone vases from Kenya. It is a reasonable expectation that water can be put in vases. In fact, the soapstone is porous and cannot hold water. We would have avoided many complaints if a simple label had been put on the vase explaining this.

The size of a product, the **material** from which it is made, the **country** where it was made, and **how it can be used** are the next items on an information check list. On some products, and in some countries, it may be a legal requirement to give some or all of these. Where it is not, it may still be important information for the consumer. Clothing requires a label indicating the size. So do large textile products, such as tablecloths, bedcovers or rugs. The material from which a product is made would invariably be included as part of the care information where this is given, because the two are obviously related. Where care information is not relevant, such as on a woodcarving or basket, it is still always worthwhile to inform the consumer about the materials from which the product has been made; not just 'wood', for example, but the particular type of wood. The indication of the country of manufacture may also sometimes be required by law. Where it is not, it is still a valuable piece of information.

A number of handicrafts require **instructions** or information about their use. For example, some of the musical instruments which Oxfam Trading imports are unknown to people in Britain. It is helpful to include a label or information sheet advising customers how to play

Robert Davis/Oxfam

By enclosing instructions and music, the exporter of this ocarina greatly increased the value and marketability of his product.

them. An exporter in Chile went further, sending us a sheet of simple tunes to play. This was very well received, as are recipes included with food products.

Oxfam Trading advises its suppliers always to label their products with the country of manufacture, the materials used, our product code number, and any other information necessary or relevant. We inform them about legal requirements in Britain. Exporters should ask themselves what information they would require if they were shopping for the product they are selling, and include that on their labels and packaging.

We also try to go beyond these basic facts to try to incorporate **information about the product and the people who made it.** This is because we are particularly interested in the cultural, technical and human aspects of handicraft production. Customers sometimes demand this. For example, we placed an order with a small co-operative in Africa, which had not exported before, for wooden sculptures, the design of which was rooted in the cultural tradition of the producers. When we put the sculptures in one of our shops, every customer who admired them asked about the meaning of the figures and about the carvers who made them. Most people were not prepared to pay the price we were asking without getting that information. They expected the product to have a label giving it. The quality of presentation of a product is inextricably linked to its value. **Good presentation increases value; poor presentation decreases it. Presentation is an integral part of the product**.

We make one further request of our suppliers. We like our name to appear on the products we sell. Oxfam is a well-known organisation in Britain, with a large number of shops. These serve other purposes, apart from selling handicrafts. By printing our name with the products we sell, we hope to attract new customers into our shops. This brand identification by retailers is a common practice. Some have their own distinctive label design, of a certain colour and style of writing, and require all labels to follow this, and may even supply the labels.

Importers have different methods of promoting their products. They would normally concentrate on the physical, emotional or other benefits to the consumer. Labels and packaging can become part of the fantasy world of advertising, in which many kinds of techniques are used to respond to and develop consumer taste. There are legal controls on what advertising and promotional materials may say. Governments are concerned that consumers should not be misled by false claims or misleading information. A system of international symbols has been introduced to provide a guarantee of the quality of a product to consumers, for example, the 'woolmark' and the mark for leather. Labels bearing these may be used by manufacturers or importers on products made of these materials. For them, it is a promotional aid; for consumers, a protection against being misled by one of the many synthetic substitutes for those materials.

The application of marks to products has gone beyond this concept to respond to other concerns of consumers. At the end of the 1970s Germany introduced a labelling scheme known as 'Blue Angel'. It was the first mark to be applied to products considered to be environmentally friendly. A manufacturer or importer wishing to use it has to provide information about the component parts and manufacturing processes of the product. Other countries have since adopted similar schemes. Another idea which was worked out first in Holland in the late 1980s is a mark to guarantee fair prices paid to producers. It was developed for trade in coffee, but subsequently also studied by ATOs in Europe for possible application to handicrafts. The motive was to respond to the growing concern among consumers about fairness and non-exploitation of poor people in international trade.

All these different pieces of information may appear either on a label or packaging. It is only certain legally required information which must be directly attached to the product in the form of a label. Which method, then, should an exporter choose? It depends on the type of product, and of course, as always, on whether the customer makes any specific request. A lot of handicrafts simply cannot be packaged, because of their size or inconvenient shape. Furniture is an obvious example. Others will sell better if not packaged, because consumers will want to touch or inspect them. For example, it is rarely worthwhile to package bags. In such cases any information must be put on a label. Where packaging is being used, one advantage is that more words can usually be written, because a package is bigger than a label.

The main purpose of packaging is **to facilitate distribution and retail sale**. Products can often be moved and stored more safely and quickly in warehouses if they are in packages. Imagine trying to handle loose puppets, for example, or mobiles. Strings and wires would be all over the place, causing havoc. Shops are able to display many products more easily and more attractively in standard size, well-designed packages. Packages allow for fuller use of space. Shop fittings enable some types of packages to hang, so that the full height of the shop is used.

Importers might specify the type of packaging which they want, because they know the way in which the product is going to be presented to consumers. There are several types of packages suitable for handicrafts. A box made of cardboard, or even of plant fibre, might be appropriate. This would hide the product from view, unless a part was cut out, or a transparent lid used. Therefore a label outside might be required, perhaps incorporating a drawing of the product, to describe it to the consumer. The sort of product for which this type of packaging might be suitable is a wooden or stone item, slightly fragile and irregular in shape. It provides protection, and enables more than one piece to be stacked on a shelf. A simple polythene bag might be sufficient to keep products clean if they are not fragile. A paper label can be stuck on the bag, or placed inside it. A common form of presentation is a card stapled to the top of a polythene bag. This serves two purposes. Information can be written on the card, and a hole can be made so that the product can hang on a shop fitting. Oxfam Trading often requests this type of packaging.

The ability to produce labels or packaging of good quality, either on your own initiative or in response to a customer's request, enhances your product, and provides a very positive promotion for your business. There are three rules to remember:

- Include only relevant information, and present it correctly. It would not, for example, be necessary to include your own company's name and address. If you are exporting, why would you want consumers overseas to know this? Write text in the language of the importer's country. Check your spelling and punctuation. An error in a label or package might imply to the consumer a defect in the product, suggesting that the production too has been careless. Spelling mistakes can have odd results. An exporter in Thailand labelled a package for a woolly lamb which we bought as 'woolly lamp'. It is easy to make errors when the language is not your own. This one was not as disastrous as that of a detergent manufacturer who decided to promote a new brand of powder by showing three pictures — on the left a pile of dirty clothes, in the centre the washing process, on the right a pile of clean clothes. The powder was promoted in the Middle East; the language duly changed to Arabic; but the exporter overlooked that reading there is from right to left.[17] The story may serve to emphasise that the package, as well as the product, must be right for the target market.

- Use labels and packaging appropriate for the product. A convenient size is a first consideration. A label as large as the product is not appropriate. Make sure the label does not damage the product. Adhesive labels can leave marks on leather, wood and stone handicrafts, for example.

- Ensure that packaging protects the product adequately. Packaging must take protection into account, because the product will be distributed inside its package. A stone carving in a box, for example, needs protective wrapping inside the box. Without it, it will move about, and movement makes breakage more likely. The amount of external packing material used will not be relevant. Products made from plant or animal materials should be packaged in polythene bags only if the bags have holes for ventilation. Otherwise moisture can cause mould to develop.

Suppliers have often misunderstood Oxfam Trading's packaging requirements. For example, we ordered a set of 12 miniature pots from South America. We wanted to sell them from our shops in a box of one dozen, in order to keep them tidy on the shelf and include some information on the box. The exporter made a wooden box of excellent quality which enabled us to distribute the pots safely from our warehouse to our shops. However, the box had to be destroyed in order to open it in the shop. The purpose of the packaging had not been served, because the supplier confused our request, thinking it was a packing requirement rather than a packaging one for retail sale. It is easy for such misunderstandings to occur.

Robert Davis/Oxfam

Oxfam Trading warehouse, Bicester. With so many different products to store and distribute, the use of code numbers on packages is essential. Extra time in the warehouse adds to costs.

Failure to supply a label indicating our code number correctly on the products we order also results from misunderstanding. We state on each order our labelling requirement, which always includes the code number on the product — if unpackaged — or on the package. Our shops need to be able to identify the products they receive from our warehouse. All of our products have code numbers as a means of identification. The code number needs to be in a visible place. A consignment of tablecloths was packaged in a polythene bag. The code number had been put on before bagging, but also before folding, with the result that it couldn't be seen, and we had to re-label the outside of the bag.

We also require the code number to appear on the outside of the export packing. This is for identification during receiving and storage procedures in our warehouse. Often, products which are not packaged are wrapped individually for protection during transportation. This wrapping will not be removed in our warehouse, because we need to send the product similarly packed to our shops. We therefore require an identifying code number label on the outside of the wrapping for our warehouse, as well as one on the actual product for our shops. It is not surprising that even experienced suppliers misunderstand this, and as a result cause us delays in our distribution process while we put on code number labels ourselves.

Exporters should ask themselves what information or promotional message about a product should be given, what is the most appropriate way to present it for retail sale, how it can travel safely and easily, and what are the special requirements of the customer. Companies selling by mail-order, like Oxfam Trading, often make additional packaging requests. Because we distribute to our mail-order customers by post, we require extra attention to be given to the safety aspect. We usually prefer products to come in strong cardboard packaging with good internal protection. Although the boxes are subsequently packed in another carton when the orders are sent out to customers, the rough handling which consignments receive in the postal system often means that light packaging is not sufficient to withstand damage. Oxfam Trading has a lot of experience of products arriving in our warehouse safely, but breaking in transit to our mail-order customers. Products sold by mail-order are generally photographed with no packaging. The text in the catalogue provides the information otherwise given on the packaging. Hence, the informational and promotional purposes of packaging are not as important as they are when products are sold in shops; whereas the safety purpose is more important.

7.2   Increasing the value of your offer

Presentation must be consistent with the use of the product, and the way it is promoted. Labels and packaging are an integral part of the product at the point of sale. The quality of them makes a direct statement to the consumer about the quality of the product itself. For example, a paper label stuck to the bottom of an expensive carved figure would be less appropriate than a cardboard label on a string around its neck. The absence of any type of label would be worse still. The consumer wants to know who or what the figure is, and the absence of this information would reduce the figure's value. A small cloth bag or paper box would be a more appropriate package for an item of jewellery than a polythene bag. If it is sold as a gift there is no need to buy additionally something to wrap it in. The consumer will therefore give a value to the package of at least as much as a sheet of gift wrapping paper.

The clear relationship between **quality of packaging** and **perception of value** of a product should be considered carefully by exporters. There might be opportunities for increasing the value of certain products by adding packaging, or improving existing packaging. Oxfam Trading gives a lot of attention to package design. For example, we sell incense sticks in long thin paper envelopes, clearly marked with the fragrance. Very few customers open the envelope to look at the sticks. They are attracted by the package rather than the product itself. When we created a more attractive package design recently, we were able to increase our selling price and thereby cover a price increase by the supplier to us, without a decrease in sales or profit margin.

Changing the packaging in this way can itself give the impression of a new product to the customer, without the need to vary the actual contents of the package. **A great deal of product differentiation occurs in this way.** Stationery products, for example, can be given a new promotion simply by changing the design on the cover. By refreshing and varying the presentation of their product, manufacturers are able to extend its life.

Soap is sold on the market in several types of package. According to the type, the image of the product changes. For example, a bar of soap in a simple polythene wrap on a supermarket shelf would be bought only for the consumer's own use. There would be strong price competition from rival soaps. Somebody wishing to buy a small gift for a friend or relation would not buy this. A soap in an attractive box would be more appropriate. Such a soap might sell for three times the price of the plain wrapped one. Yet the buyer would be happy because the good quality of the packaging is an essential part of the message conveyed by the gift. The actual cost of production of the more expensive soap would not be three times more than that of the cheaper. It would probably contain more perfume, but basically the same ingredients. A box would, of course, cost more than the polythene wrap, but not by the amount that the selling prices reflect. Skilful packaging may thus increase value and **position a product in the gift market**. By permitting an increase in the selling price which is greater than the additional cost of the packaging, this will increase profit margins. Consumers pay happily in order to solve their problem of what to buy someone as a gift.

Adding labels or printing words on packaging in order to create a promotional message can also allow for imaginative additions of value. For example, woven bracelets have been promoted by exporters in both Guatemala and India as friendship — or *amigo* (Spanish for friend) — bands. A story on the package describes the idea of wearing it to show friendship. This is successful marketing, selling an attractive idea — being friendly — around a product. The additional value of the packaged bracelet over an unpackaged one, just sold as a simple bracelet, is greater than the cost of providing the material on which the idea is described.

Robert Davis/Oxfam

Amigo band: the value of this simple bracelet is greatly enhanced by a marketing promotion associating it with the idea of friendship.

One difficulty may be the availability and cost of materials suitable for labels and packaging in producing countries. However, a virtue can often be made out of necessity by **using handicrafts themselves as packaging materials**. For example, soaps and other small items can be packaged in a small bag, made of locally printed cloth, or in a basket. With the addition of a little attractive packaging material, like coloured tissue paper, you can again make a very successful gift, in which the additional value added to the products will be greater than the additional cost. An exporter in Colombia achieved very large sales for many years, selling small baskets to the USA, where consumers bought them as a package for gifts. In India, a producer group makes small hand-made paper boxes, which serve the same purpose.

Oxfam Trading sold successfully for many years a small basket of spices from Grenada in the Caribbean. Seven local unground spices were packed into a basket, also made on the island. A label was attached, giving some recipes. Combining products in this way can enable a price to be charged which is in excess of the total of the parts individually. The spice basket now became an attractive gift, and could be sold very profitably. Stationery items offer similar possibilities. Writing paper and envelopes, and perhaps cards, can be sold in folders, and thereby be more suitable as a gift.

Labels can also be made by hand, though not in very large quantities. It might be possible to design an attractive label, written by hand, on good quality paper or card. That it is not done more often is probably due more to lack of awareness of its usefulness than to lack of manual capacity.

Another way in which a change of presentation can increase the value of a product is the identification of a **different use** for it. An important promotional advantage of handicrafts is that they can often be used in various ways. **Their use in the importing country may not be the same as that in the country of production.** For example, hanging baskets made of jute and cane have been exported in huge numbers from Bangladesh. They were used traditionally for keeping food safely stored off the ground, away from rodents and insects. Although they would not be marketed for that purpose overseas, they have, instead, been sold as hanging plant holders, to decorate the house. Oxfam Trading has sold many hanging baskets in this way. Occasionally we change the presentation in order to keep the offer to the customer fresh. We have shown the same baskets used to hold vegetables in the kitchen, and toiletries in the bathroom. We are, in effect, thinking for our customers. They might be reluctant to buy another hanging basket for somebody who already has one with a plant in it; but not if they can say that the new one is for a different purpose. In this way, we can maintain demand and hold off the normal decline of the product cycle.

Similarly, we succeeded in giving new life to a magazine rack by showing it in our mail-order catalogue in subsequent years as a record holder, and then, put on its side, as a filing tray. In the latter presentation, it was a huge success because of the originality of the idea. We have shown identical pieces of cloth as bedcovers, tablecloths and throws for the decoration of a settee. Our customers have come to look to us for selling not only new products, but new ideas for the use of handicrafts.

Identifying or creating a use for what is essentially a decorative product has provided the inspiration for other successful handicraft product development. Oxfam Trading sold carved wooden statues from Malawi, adapted as lampbases. The only alteration required was to create a channel through which an electric wire could be fitted, and to flatten the head so that the light fitting could be screwed in. The electrical attachments were put on in Britain in order to comply with safety standards. The product was more valuable for both looking beautiful and having a useful purpose in the British market. Designers have created belts, bags, clothing and soft furnishings from traditional

Oxfam Trading

Promoting different uses for the same product in successive years keeps the product 'fresh' for customers and maintains demand.

pieces of textile work, consistent with the best formula for export handicraft design: **adapting what is traditional in the country of production to the taste in the country of sale.**

A handicraft is an individual creation. No opportunity should be lost to promote that fact. In Chile and Peru women make cloth pictures from scrap material, known as *arpilleras*. On the back can often be found a little pocket, containing a piece of paper on which the woman has written her name and perhaps the title of the picture. This thoughtful detail increases the value of the product, by upgrading it to **an individual piece of art, created by a named artist.** Oxfam Trading always suggests to suppliers that as many products as possible be signed in some way. Customers greatly appreciate the identification of the actual producer. It is part of the appeal of handicrafts as an individual, human activity, unlike the repetitive mechanical one of industrial production.

Robert Davis/Oxfam

Arpillera: the maker signed her name, so the customer appreciates it as a work of art.

122

Labels and packaging are useful not only for distributing products safely and in compliance with legal requirements. They are important promotional tools. Their use needs to be understood by exporters if they are to get the most value out of their offer, and distinguish themselves from competitors selling similar products.

7.3   Pricing

I remember a handicraft producer once telling me, 'Each one of my products has four prices. First, there is the one I charge to my regular local customers. That's the lowest price. My second price is a bit higher, and that's for well-to-do visitors from the city. I have a third price, higher still, for foreign tourists. And my highest price of all is for the specially rich foreign tourists who stay in the best hotels.'

This producer had a pricing policy related to his understanding of how much each particular market was prepared to pay. Any producer knows that if you price your articles too high, nobody will buy them. What is too high? It means above the value which a market is prepared to accord to a product, with regard to the usefulness of the product, the quality of its presentation, and the price of similar products offered by competitors. **Price is ultimately determined by the market place**, and the right price at which to sell products is the highest price you can obtain without adversely affecting sales levels.

The difficulty with pricing for export is that it is not easy to obtain the information you need about the market's perception of the value of your product. As in the domestic market, it may be different among the potential customers. For example, a specialist importer of wood carvings, with customers looking for high-quality distinctive sculptures, might well be prepared to pay more for such pieces than a general handicraft importer with more downmarket outlets. However, it is not good policy to offer samples of the same products to different buyers at different prices, even if you think their perception of value will be different. For, unlike selling in the producing country, **export marketing has to be more structured and more consistent**. Prices are not arrived at by bargaining face to face, as in a local market place. An exporter cannot test out each importer's maximum price. The onus is on the exporter to make an offer to an importer, who will normally take time to consider it. Although there can be correspondence about the price of a product, it does not usually put the exporter in a good light to alter prices just because the buyer wants to negotiate. That would remove confidence in the prices of the other products. And you certainly cannot invite customers to pay a bit more if they can afford to!

The usual method of communicating prices to potential buyers is to publish a price list. **This should be valid for all customers, and for a certain length of time**. It is necessary to maintain prices for a reasonable period, which should usually be not less than six months. There is often a delay of some months between making an offer to an importer and receiving an order. Clearly, the importer is not going to be pleased if, after the order has been placed, it is then returned by the exporter, requesting extra payment because of a price increase. However, if this does happen for any reason, the exporter would obviously be in a much better position if able to point out to the customer that the order was sent after the expiry date of the price list, which the customer can verify. An example of bad pricing practice was an African exporter who sent a sample to an importer, and received a very large order. The exporter thought that if the customer wanted the product so badly, the price could be increased. The customer, receiving the notification, promptly cancelled the order.

Importers expect that export prices have been based on accurate costing of the product. If this is so, then there is little room for negotiation. Pricing needs to be based on the cost of a product and the overheads of the business in order for the exporter to be satisfied that these are being adequately covered, and that some profit remains for investment in the business. For an exporter who buys a finished product from a producer, or another trader, the starting point is the price paid. An exporter who is also the producer must calculate the cost of production.

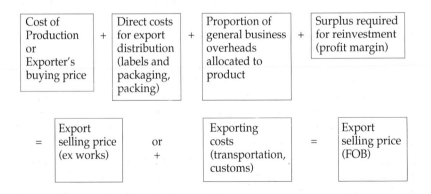

Fig. 19: *Calculation of export selling price based on product costing*

The selling price should then be checked against estimates of the best price available in the market. It might be possible to edge it up on some products, or necessary to reduce it a little on others. **The correct approach to pricing is to cost the product accurately, and then adjust according to what you think the market will bear.**

What if the market will not pay the price which you calculate you need in order to recover the costs of making — or buying — the product, distributing it, recovering your overheads and making a small surplus? There are two courses of possible action. The first is to see if costs can be cut in any way at any stage of the production and distribution process, or the selling price increased, perhaps by changing the marketing mix. The second is to look at your costing in more detail, separating the direct costs of production and distribution from the indirect costs of running the business and making a surplus. Many businesses are rather inflexible in their approach, adding a fixed percentage to their production cost — or buying price — which overall keeps them solvent. This is known as 'cost-plus pricing'. Yet it might be possible to sell profitably at a lower price which at least recovers the direct costs.

For example, a basket manufacturer has a production cost of 20 and normally adds 40 per cent to arrive at an ex works export price. Over the years, this percentage has kept the business going, with enough surplus for the owners to live on. The normal selling price, then, is 28. However, new competition enters the market, and orders dry up. Could the manufacturer afford to drop the price to 25? Perhaps. If the direct costs are only 3, and the proportion of overheads and profit allocated to the product 5, then the price could be reduced. The consequence depends on what happens to sales volume. If it stays the same as before, then the overall profitability of the business will decline. If it increases, the actual cash — rather than percentage — profitability may increase.

The method of pricing which is based on recovery of direct costs only is known as 'pricing to make a contribution to overheads'. It is a more flexible method, which can serve exporters well. For example, it would allow them to test out the relationship on a product between price and demand, by reducing the price, perhaps for a trial period. It would permit a discount scheme to be introduced, for large orders. It might also allow an exporter to continue selling a product which has a special importance, even though it yields a lower profit margin than other products. What matters is that, overall, **the business recovers its total overheads and makes a small surplus**. It does not actually matter whether the contribution of each product in the range is equal or not. Oxfam Trading applies this policy. We import certain products to which we can add a lower margin than normal, because it is important to us to continue supporting the producers of them. They still make a contribution to our overheads, and we earn enough on other products to balance our books at the end of the year.

Pricing, then, consists partly of the **science of costing**, and partly of the **art of promotion**. It is a key component of the total offer, and, like the other parts, must be approached creatively, and in relation to the rest of the offer. It must be able to adapt to a change in presentation, or promotion, or competition. There is a saying in India that a loaf of bread is worthless in a feast, but priceless in a famine. It costs the same to produce for either.

Oxfam Trading's experience is that costing and pricing are weak areas of many small handicraft businesses. Costs are sometimes overlooked, or misunderstood. Profitability can be damaged by an increase in production costs — perhaps due to a price rise in raw materials. You should try to make some allowance for this when calculating costs, if working with a material of which the price is fairly unstable. A price list should always state the basis of the prices and make clear what the standard product packaging is. If a customer wishes to have something additional, then it is reasonable to charge for the cost of that. A small request which costs very little to comply with — perhaps to apply code numbers to each product — should not be charged for. It is good customer relations to have enough allowance in the prices to be able to absorb small additional production or packaging costs during the period of validity of the price list.

The relationship of domestic prices to export prices is one that is treated differently among handicraft businesses. There are inevitably additional costs in exporting, if you do it on an FOB basis. There might, however, be an export incentive which you could claim, which would more than cover those costs. Some economies of scale might be possible in producing the larger volume of most export orders, allowing for a reduction in prices. Some businesses undertake all their exports on a contribution basis, in order to keep prices low, while recovering their overheads fully in domestic sales. Most importers would find it strange if the export price were higher than the domestic one. It is general practice in trade that price is in a relationship with volume, and that **the larger the order, the lower the price**. A number of exporters offer price reductions either for large quantities of a product, or for an order with an overall high value. Prices of some handicrafts are controlled by a 'floor price', below which they may not be exported. This is a system imposed usually by an exporting country, in order to maintain quality standards and export revenues.

Export contracts should always be made in a **hard currency**, preferably, for the customer's convenience, that of the importing country, or US dollars. This is the only way in which exporters can be protected against devaluation of their currency. For example, suppose 100 local currency units buy $1 at the time an exporter accepts an order. It takes four months to produce. By the time it is paid by the customer, there has been inflation of 25 per cent and devaluation of 20 per cent. A product sold at $1 will bring in 120 local currency units, which nearly covers the inflation. Assuming materials had been bought early on, the exporter would probably not lose out. Suppose, though, that the contract had been made in local currency. At the time of payment, 100 units would be received: good news for the customer, who now only has to send 80 cents to buy those 100 local currency units, but very bad news for the exporter, whose costs have risen 25 per cent but whose income remained static. More than one inexperienced exporter has been caught out in this way.

If the levels of inflation and currency devaluation stay roughly in line, export prices in hard currency can remain stable. Prices from many countries used to remain unchanged for several years. Nowadays this is less common. Inflation of very high levels in handicraft producing countries has sometimes been accompanied by fixed exchange rates imposed by their governments. When this happens, the amount of local currency received does not keep up with increasing costs of production. There is then little alternative to increasing export prices.

Summary

1 Presentation of your product is an integral part of the overall offer. Labels and packaging fulfil requirements to provide information about the safety of a product, and its care when in use. They also offer considerable promotional opportunities. New labels are being developed in line with growing consumer concerns, such as environmental consequences of production, and fair trade. Packaging plays an important role in distribution and retail display. Labels and packaging are insufficiently used by most handicraft exporters.

2 Packaging can enable an exporter to move a product into the gift market, and thereby add value. Handicrafts themselves can be used as packaging. Identifying new uses for products can also increase their value, and extend their life. Sometimes this involves product

development, adding a function to a decorative product. Use any possible opportunity to promote handicrafts as individual pieces of art, in order to increase their value.

3 Pricing consists partly of the science of costing, and partly of the art of promotion. An inflexible approach based on costs might lead to lost market opportunities. Pricing based on making a contribution to overheads and profit allows exporters to vary their price in relation to their overall offer. It is important to quote export prices in hard currency, to protect yourself against devaluation of your own currency.

8 FULFILLING ORDERS

8.1 Supplying to specification

There are eight main features of any export order. The order must be checked to ensure they are all included, they are clear and that the order can be fulfilled according to specification.

The product

An exporter of sisal cord received an order for 1,000 metres of cord 'as per sample enclosed'. In order to ensure that the exact specification was followed, a small sample length had been sent with the order. To the importer's horror, the exporter duly sent the 1,000 metres, cut into pieces exactly the same length as the sample.

Handicraft export trade is fraught with such misunderstandings. There are many times when the same words can communicate two different things to the exporter and importer. 'Deliver by June' perhaps means that the goods should leave the country of production in June, or arrive in the country of destination then. Neither party realises there is a misunderstanding until it is too late to avoid a problem. Very often difficulties occur because the importer has left details insufficiently clear on the order.

Oxfam Trading has encountered a lot of difficulty over garment sizes. It is not sufficient to place an order for 'large' or 'medium' unless there is a detailed specification from the supplier of the measurements of chest, length and sleeve length of each size. Other difficulties occur because the supplier fails to communicate the full specification of a product when sending a sample. For example, a bag might always be sold in assorted colours. An importer receiving one sample and not knowing about other colours might assume that the order will be supplied only in that colour, and might have a problem if it is not. An importer — particularly an inexperienced one — might simply fail to understand the importance of a detail of the product specification. It might seem unimportant in an assortment of Christmas tree

ABC IMPORT LIMITED
1 Snow Lane
London EC1X 2CY
Tel: 071 236 5142
Fax: 071 285 6131

ORDER NUMBER A 5200

DATE 13th March, 1991

TO: Handicraft Co-Operative Export Ltd
      PO Box 385
      Mbabane
      Swaziland

PLEASE SUPPLY AS PER THE FOLLOWING INSTRUCTIONS

OUR PRODUCT CODE NO.	QUANTITY	PRODUCT DESCRIPTION	UNIT PRICE
SW 6834	150	Round basket, 10" your ref.BS3	$5.25
SW 6835	100	Nesting S/2 baskets your ref.BS6	$8.50
DE 6839	150	Oblong basket, 10" your ref.BS9	$6.00
SW 4160	30	Royal Swazi necklace	$8.50
SW 4161	50	" bracelet	$4.50
SW4162	50	" earrings	$3.50

LABELS & PACKAGING: Our code number to appear on each item. All outers to be marked with code number and quantity per box.

PRICE BASIS: FOB

PAYMENT TERMS: Cash against documents

METHOD OF SHIPMENT: Sea freight

SHIPMENT DATE: To arrive UK by October 1st, 1991

DOCUMENTS REQUIRED: Invoice (3 copies), Packing list (3 copies), Original B/L, GSP Form A.

PLEASE CONFIRM ORDER PROMPTLY
INTERNATIONAL INSURANCE COVERED BY ABC IMPORT LTD
SEE SEPARATE DOCUMENT FOR FORWARDING INSTRUCTIONS

Fig. 20: *Details to be included on an export order*

decorations exactly which designs are included in a pack of six. The importer may, however, have specified to omit Father Christmas and Snowman, because these designs have already been bought in selections from other suppliers.

Supplying to specification means, first, understanding in detail the **precise requirement of the customer**, and then exercising **strict quality control** so that what is sent matches it. The more production is dispersed, the more potential there is for variations in production. In general, **quality control standards in handicraft export trade need to be improved**. In Oxfam Trading's experience, as much difficulty can arise from communication breakdowns as because of slack supervision by the exporter. For example, we received the following letter in response to an order placed with a supplier in Thailand: [18]

> 'What was not understood clearly was the references to colours. Although we do have colour code numbers as well as names of colours in our catalogue, your order does not conform to either of these and our staff were at a loss to know exactly what you required. For example, they had not the faintest idea what colour 'fawn' is. I presume you mean 'beige'. This was further confusing for them because your item 019186 is described as being BK (Black?)/FAWN and requesting the colours blue and green!! Our staff thought fawn was either blue or green. Thus, when fawn is mentioned in 019160 and 019232, they thought fawn must be either green or blue. Again, people here do not drink 'wine' (see 019178) and do not associate 'burgundy' with anything. Later, in 019194, we are asked for 'wine' and they were not sure what colour 'wine' was because if you had wanted 'burgundy', as in 019178, you would have asked for it. Confused?
>
> What I am trying to get at is that using codes and colour names known to the producers and in their catalogue will help them to make what is required. Even now, we are not certain what is required by you for No. 019186. Production may be held up.'

When a misunderstanding is realised, or when a detail in an order is not clear, the obvious thing to do is to contact the customer to explain it and await clarification before proceeding with production. It is when the misunderstanding is not realised that there is likely to be a problem. We ordered some jumpsuits from Africa in blue cloth that had been sampled to us. However, the cloth was not available when production took place. The producer did inform us before sending them that the suits had been made in green cloth 'but they look very nice and we're sure you'll sell them'. The item was featured in a page of blue clothing in our mail-order catalogue, and the change of colour was very problematic for us. It often happens that product specifications do have to change because materials become unavailable between the time of sending a sample and placing an order. If that occurs, **you must contact the customer**, and await the reply before producing.

Labels and packaging

Probably the single biggest shortfall in fulfilment of Oxfam Trading's orders is labelling with our code number on the product, and, additionally where applicable, on protective packaging. Our Goods In Department has to put these on if the supplier does not, because the warehouse system cannot function unless products bear their code number. At times of peak operation, in October and November, consignments can be seriously delayed in moving from the receiving bay to the order-picking shelves because the Goods In procedure is slowed down by the need to label. Importers do not include labelling requirements in orders just to make work for exporters. **A request has its purpose**. If there is a difficulty in complying with it, the importer should be informed. Where labels are required by law because of a safety standard, the importer would again have to put these on if the exporter failed to. There could be a further delay in getting them printed, because the need was not anticipated.

The type of packaging difficulty which we experience most often is that related to units of distribution. We might ask for a product to be packaged in fours, sixes, or dozens because that is the unit in which we want to distribute the product from our warehouse to our shops. The unit might be a display box, in which the products will stay on the shop shelf, or simply a disposable bag or box which contains the right number of products. If the products arrive packaged in a different way it again causes extra work — and hence delay and expense — in our warehouse. This is a common area of confusion, because suppliers do not understand our system of distribution. Hence, they do not give sufficient importance to the details of the packaging instruction. Sometimes customers make unreasonable requests, perhaps demanding boxes where these are difficult and expensive to obtain. We once ordered 5,000 glass bottles, containing pictures made of sand, from Brazil. We requested that they be packed in a boxed unit of one dozen so that we could distribute that quantity to each of our shops. The supplier, mindful above all else of the safety aspect of transporting glass bottles, did not comply with our request. Instead, the bottles were sent in cartons, with corrugated dividers between each bottle. 4,998 arrived safely; it was an excellent effort. Our own request had been inappropriate; there would have been much more chance of breakage if the bottles had been packed into small boxes without dividers. Still, even when the customer is wrong, the exporter should write to explain why the packaging supplied will be different.

Price

An export contract must always state in which currency the price is stated and the basis of the price: ex works, FOB (stating from where) or other. If it does not, there is the possibility of a misunderstanding and subsequent argument. Prices can change between sending a sample and receiving an order, or fulfilling one order and receiving a subsequent one. If the price on the order is not correct, or satisfactory, **the customer must be advised at once**. A supplier in Africa failed to send us an order for carpets because the price had been increased significantly owing to the escalating cost of wool. Rather than inform us and try to negotiate a new price, it was assumed that we would not agree, and production did not start. Not hearing about the difficulty, we included the carpet in our mail-order catalogue, and disappointed all our customers by not supplying their orders. It has happened more than once that suppliers have fulfilled an order at a loss because they didn't want to advise us of a price increase in case we were annoyed, or cancelled the order. We do not want to exploit a supplier by paying an unreasonably low price. If the price put on an order is not acceptable, the customer must be advised, with an explanation. **If the reason is fair, and the increase modest, the customer is likely to accept it**. After all, any competitors have probably had to increase prices similarly. It is not good practice to change a price between the time of accepting an order and fulfilling it, and in no circumstances without informing the customer. There may be exceptional reasons why it is necessary to change a price after production has started, but doing so would not be at all well received by a customer, who might refuse to pay it.

Quantity

The quantity ordered needs checking first against the production capacity and delivery date. Is it possible to make the amount requested within the time allowed? If not, the customer should be advised approximately how many would be made, or how long it would take to complete the total quantity ordered. The quantity should then be checked against the price in case there is any price variation according to quantity ordered or value of order. Finally, it needs checking for clarity. Sets can cause confusion. Does '500 plant pots, sets of 5', mean 500 or 2,500? The unit in the quantity column should always agree with the unit in the price column. If the price of a set of five plant pots has been put in the price column, then the quantity which the customer is ordering refers to sets. But Oxfam Trading has been caught out by such confusion more than once, receiving a much larger quantity than we had meant to order.

Payment

An order should also state the **method and timing of payment**. It is helpful to be flexible on terms of payment. An importer may have a preference for a particular method, which might be different from the exporter's normal method, but quite acceptable. The exporter's concerns are speed and safety: to receive money promptly and fully. If a customer places an order with payment terms that are not acceptable, then the exporter must advise of this and suggest alternative ones.

Delivery date

Importers plan their delivery dates with considerable care. They must make allowance for cash flow, warehouse space and selling seasons. For example, if Oxfam Trading places an order for a product which will be featured in our Spring mail-order catalogue, we want to receive it in December or January, as will be stated on the order. Any earlier or later will cause us difficulty. We have financial commitments and limited space in our warehouse at the peak selling season of October and November. If the products arrive later than January, they will not be in stock at the time we start selling from our catalogue, so that we could not fulfil our customers' orders.

   The delivery date is as important a detail as any other on an order. If an exporter foresees difficulty in complying with it, immediate contact should be made with the customer. It happens very often that production is planned to comply with the required date, but something unforeseen goes wrong before shipment, perhaps with production, perhaps with shipping arrangements. Vessels do not always respect their planned sailing dates, for example. If the importer is informed, there is a chance that alternative arrangements could be made satisfactorily, or that, if a delay is unavoidable, the importer can advise customers if necessary. To deliver later than required without previous warning is very bad customer relations. Exporters are sometimes under pressure to fulfil an order early because the producers want to be paid. The consignment should be sent early only after obtaining permission from the importer for a change in this condition of the order.

Late delivery is an even bigger problem than early delivery. If a product is seasonal, or a promotion of it is limited, and it arrives late, the importer cannot sell it. Oxfam Trading has this problem every year with its mail-order catalogues. A catalogue is a promotion with a fixed life, unlike a retail outlet open every day. At the end of the Summer or Christmas seasons, a catalogue finishes. If stock arrives after the end of the season, there is no means of selling it. It will have to be disposed of in some other way, probably at a reduced price. Or it may be re-offered in a future catalogue, at the expense of another product. The exporter may in this way lose another order which would otherwise have been made. One late delivery, preceded by a reasonable explanation, might be accepted by an importer. Persistent lateness will quickly gain an exporter a bad reputation, and threaten future orders.

Method of shipment

The importer will advise the required method of shipment, on the order. This will have been calculated with respect to the size of the consignment, the level of urgency of delivery, and the routes available between the exporting and importing countries. If an importer requests a consignment to be sent by sea freight, and it is sent by air at great extra cost, there is likely to be an argument. Conversely, if an order is placed for delivery by air freight because it is required quickly, and the exporter despatches it by sea, there could be problems. Exporters do sometimes despatch by air freight against the customer's instruction, claiming it is quicker and safer. The real reason may be that they want to be paid more quickly. This would be very bad customer relations: an importer who is obliged to pay higher costs because the terms of the order have not been followed is likely to be extremely annoyed. **The exporter has no right to change the stated method of shipment without consultation.**

Nevertheless there can be a good reason for an exporter to suggest a better arrangement than the importer has stated. It may be that a special air freight rate might be available that would make a consignment more economical than by sea. Sea freight is logistically very difficult from some land-locked countries. It would be irresponsible for an exporter not to suggest a better option just because the importer was unaware of it. The situation regarding international freight is changing all the time. An exporter should keep up to date with developments and inform customers when there is an advantageous alternative.

Documents

An order should also state **the documents which the importer requires** to accompany the consignment. On receiving an order, an exporter should check that they are all available; and on despatching the consignment, ensure that they are all sent. Some are produced by the exporter — the invoice and packing list. The transportation document — airway bill or bill of lading — will be obtained by the freight forwarder. Others — notably the Certificate of Origin — are supplied by a government office. If a document is requested which is not known to the exporter, and appears not to be available, the importer must be advised. It may be that it is not essential, but failure to produce an essential document will cause serious problems to the importer. Documents must be not only complete, but also timely. Every year, Oxfam Trading pays a number of storage — or demurrage — bills to shipping companies and airlines, who will not release a consignment until they have received documents and clearance of goods by British Customs. This is a terribly frustrating waste of money. If a consignment is sent by air freight it will reach its destination in a very few days. It is not sufficient to send the relevant documents by post. The must either accompany the consignment or be sent separately by courier.

Importers are sometimes careless in the preparation of their orders, and exporters careless in reading them. A problem may arise which could have been solved by timely communication. **Understanding the importance of the details is the pre-requisite for fulfilling an order according to the importer's specifications.**

8.2 Keeping in touch with the customer

Communication with customers should take place at three levels. First, there is some essential communication about **orders**. Second, you will need some ongoing **sales promotion** with the objective of getting more orders. This includes responding to requests from customers for new samples. Third, there will be **general information and news** which either customers might need or like to know, or which you might want to obtain from them. For the most part, this communication will take place by correspondence. For sales promotion and information exchange, visits are much more effective. Even if it is never or only rarely possible to visit, the important thing is to **keep in touch**. You need to find out two things about your customers as quickly as possible:

- their procedures and timetables for making buying decisions;
- the information they like to receive.

In addition to this particular information, which might well be different for each customer, you need to keep all customers informed about anything which affects your offer, such as changes in prices or new product development.

Oxfam Trading, for example, is making buying decisions all the year round. We are happy to receive new samples at any time, especially when it is possible to take advantage of saving costs by including them in shipments of orders. Other importers might buy only at specific times and want to receive new samples only then. Because of our trading philosophy, we are always interested in receiving information about and photographs of the producers of the products we buy. Other importers might not be so interested. Build up a **profile of each customer** in order to respond best to the particular interest of each one. It might be useful to keep a calendar wallchart in the office, as a reminder of which customers need to be contacted, when during the year, about what. Keeping up regular communications with individual customers gives you the best chance of receiving back from them the information you want, such as reaction to samples, and the sales performance of your products.

Communication about orders should be maintained until the production is completed in accordance with the specification. The first vital response to the receipt of an order is the **confirmation**. The customer must be advised as quickly as possible that the order can be fulfilled, or consulted about any problem with it. A customer should sign an order, and the supplier should sign a confirmation. In that way, it becomes a contract, with each party holding the copy signed by the other. This is why it is important that **all details are checked carefully at the time of receiving an order**. After receiving your signed confirmation, the customer is under no obligation to accept any modification. If there are any problems in accepting any of the conditions of the order, it is much better to write a separate letter, rather than simply send a confirmation with a detail altered. This is to ensure that the customer is made aware of the change; an alteration might otherwise be missed. The customer also needs to have an explanation of why you cannot fulfil the order exactly as specified.

Oxfam Trading often has problems of discrepancies between the specifications of orders and the fulfilment of them. Many could be avoided by an advice from the supplier, at the time of receiving an order, that some aspect is problematic. You should not be hesitant about querying an order with a customer, if this is necessary. For example, a supplier in South America refused to supply an order for 100 wallhangings all of the same design, saying that to do so would undermine artistic creativity. Another told us that a basket could not be made of a uniform size because the concept of standardisation was not yet understood by producers of very limited commercial experience. There is no difficulty about this kind of objection, if the customer has time to re-plan. What you should not do is leave the customer expecting that the specifications of the order will be met, when in fact it is not possible. That this happens so often is due to the lack of appreciation by inexperienced exporters of the importance of all the details. They often read just the quantities, description and price, and start producing.

An order may be confirmed in any convenient way. Oxfam Trading always sends an extra copy of the order, for the exporter to return to us. A number of exporters send a proforma invoice (see Figure 21). This is not a request for payment, but rather a record on the supplier's own stationery of all the details of the order. The customer is usually then asked to further sign and retain a copy. Alternatively, a simple letter, or quicker means of written communication if necessary, can be sent. International trade often requires quick communication. Electronic mail is a technical innovation of the late 1980s which offers speed and cheapness, using computers and telephone lines. Prior to its wide adoption the best system available almost everywhere is the fax. If an exporting business does not have its own fax machine, then it should make an arrangement with an office which does, in order to be able to receive and send faxes. They speed up communication at times when it is important to do so. For example, Oxfam Trading sends orders out by fax if they are urgent, or if the postal service to the country concerned is slow. Confirmations can be sent back by fax. Telexes may also be used, but are only for textual messages. The fax reproduces any document exactly, and so is ideal for orders or proforma invoices. Original documents can be sent on by post.

When confirming an order, it is a good idea to send details about **transportation costs**. If a customer is ordering for the first time, this information will probably be appreciated. Importers like to know as accurately as possible what their total costs will be when buying a product. This could be particularly relevant when despatching by air

HANDICRAFT CO-OPERATIVE EXPORT LTD.
(HANDCOOPEX)
P.O.BOX 385
MBABANE
SWAZILAND

Telephone and Fax: 48326   Telex: 2413

PROFORMA INVOICE

To ABC Import Ltd.
1 Snow Lane
London EC1X 2CY
A5200

DATE 28th March, 1991

CUSTOMER ORDER NO.

YOUR PRODUCT CODE NO.	QUANTITY	ARTICLE	UNIT PRICE FOB US$	TOTAL US$
SW 6834	150	Round basket, 10"	5.25	787.50
SW 6835	100	Nesting S/2 baskets	8.50	850.00
SW 6839	150	Oblong basket, 10"	6.00	900.00
SW 4160	30	Royal Swazi necklace	8.50	255.00
SW 4161	50	Royal Swazi bracelet	4.50	225.00
SW 4162	50	Royal Swazi earring	3.50	175.00

TOTAL VALUE OF ORDER US$ 3192.50

LABELS/PACKAGING: All items to carry code number

PACKING: Export cartons/banded. Contents marked on box.

DOCUMENTS: Original Invoice stating Goods Inspected
Packing List
Original Bill of Lading
GSP Form A

INSURANCE: To your account

SHIPPING: Sea freight

SHIPPING DATE: To arrive UK by October 1st, 1991

PAYMENT: Cash against documents

FOR: HANDCOOPEX

Signature...................

FOR: ABC Import Ltd.

Signature..................

Fig.21: *A proforma invoice confirming an order.*

139

freight, because there is so much variation in air freight rates from country to country.

While the order is in production, importers appreciate news about its progress. If everything is proceeding according to schedule, and delivery will be on time, then there is no need to write to say only this. However, when there is another reason for contacting a customer it is always worth mentioning how production is proceeding. **It is when there is a problem that it is really important to contact the customer**. In Oxfam Trading's experience, too few exporters do this. It is as if they are reluctant to upset the customer with bad news. Yet the customer is going to be much more upset not to be told, when there might still be time to make alternative plans. We spend a lot of time and money contacting suppliers in order to get information about orders which are overdue.

All sorts of difficulties can interfere with planning in handicraft production, such as the supply of materials, a change in the weather, an organisational problem in a production unit, or a personal difficulty encountered by a producer. Such things might affect your ability to supply according to the specification in a number of ways. You might want to substitute a colour, reduce the quantity, or deliver late, for example. Always keep your customer informed, and consult on any necessary changes. Use the telex or fax when speed of communication is important. **Communication is part of the service which you must offer your customers**, and the quality of your service is as important as the quality of your products. Communication breeds confidence in a relationship between two businesses in different countries; confidence can be destroyed if communication is lacking.

Remember always to give **full and clear information**. Oxfam Trading sometimes receives messages from suppliers advising that a consignment will be late. What we want to know is — how late? When will it arrive? We ourselves were once made to suffer the consequences of an unclear communication we sent to a supplier. Chasing an order, we telexed 'Re. order no...., please hasten delivery'. The supplier interpreted 're. order' as meaning we wanted another order, instead of 'with reference to order', and made double the quantity! The fax is very helpful in enabling fuller communication to be sent quickly, at relatively low cost, reducing the risk of unclear communications.

8.3   Packing for export

There is nothing more disappointing — and more costly — than receiving a consignment into our warehouse, only to discover that the products are damaged because of inadequate packing. All the effort and money spent in producing them, and then shipping them a great distance across the world, is worthless. In the export process, **adequate packing is as important as producing to specification and quality control**. If an exporter is not sufficiently experienced or resourced to undertake it, then it is best to contract the work to a professional packing company. Freight forwarders sometimes have packing departments.

Packing has the objective of transporting a consignment safely and economically to the importer. There are five considerations:

Protection against breakage

Breakage usually occurs for one of three reasons:

- Pressure exerted from outside when the packages are stacked in transit. Perhaps other heavy packages are put on top, or pushed alongside; perhaps a packer sits on them!
- Impact from rough handling. Packages are unfortunately thrown or dropped by handlers all too often.
- Vibration in transit, especially during road transportation in the country of production.

It is essential to try to minimise the adverse consequences of these, because it is impossible to stop them happening. There are four fundamental rules:

- All products which are not packaged require some form of protective wrapping. Fragile materials must be especially protected in an appropriate way. Obviously some materials are especially fragile, such as ceramics — especially low-fired ones — or stoneware. These particularly, but all products to some extent, must be well wrapped, and protected from knocking against one another. There are several types of wrapping material commonly available, such as shredded paper, wood chippings, or plastic bubble wrap. Oxfam Trading received wooden sculptures from Tanzania without any form of wrapping inside the box. Several were broken, or marked where they had knocked against one other. Stone carvings

Robert Davis/Oxfam

All the care put into making a product is wasted if it is damaged when it arrives.

from Kenya suffered damage because some pieces were wrapped only in paper, which gave insufficient protection.

- Particular care should be taken to avoid stress on weak points in a product. Some designs are vulnerable, for example animals with protruding ears, trunks or tails. Handles of cups, bowls and vases can break easily. Any such parts need special wrapping.

- Movement of products has to be avoided. Much breakage occurs from the shock when products knock against each other. If all individual pieces are properly wrapped, and packed so tightly that no movement is possible, then maximum protection will be given. Oxfam Trading imported ceramic plant pots from Mexico, packed in a cardboard box. This also contained a saucer, which was part of the product. The pots arrived safely but many of their saucers broke, because inside the box they were not adequately protected from knocking against the pot.

- The outer container needs to be sufficiently strong to withstand pressure applied from the outside. If cardboard cartons are used, then they must be of an adequate thickness. There are other possibilities such as wooden crates, but these are suitable only for sea freight. They would be too expensive to use for air freight, because of their weight. In containerised shipping, outer cartons also need to be of adequate quality to withstand pressure from stacking.

Robert Davis/Oxfam

An example of good packing, protecting a fragile product.

Protection against climate

International transportation can subject consignments to severe temperatures, both hot and cold, and changes between them, and to changes in moisture levels. Packages might be left outside in docks or airports, exposed to heat or rain. Inside a freight forwarder's shed, they might be subject to high temperatures; in the hold of an aeroplane to low ones. Packing therefore needs to take into account any possible adverse consequences. The major difficulty is a **combination of heat and moisture**, which combine to encourage bacteria and fungi. These attack materials and cause weakness and staining. To avoid these problems, follow four rules:

- If any materials might contain moisture, dry them out properly before packing. Wood which might not have been properly seasoned is subject to staining, as well as cracking. For example, Oxfam Trading received a consignment of painted wooden animals from Indonesia, all covered with a white mould.

- In storage before packing, try to avoid severe changes of temperatures. Give consideration to the building materials used for storage sheds, and also ventilation. When a store is hot in the day and cold at night, condensation occurs which can get on to and inside packages.

- Do not put products which could contain moisture into sealed plastic bags. Allow air to enter and moisture to escape by punching holes in the bags. Oxfam Trading received a consignment of baskets from Peru which had been packed while damp inside sealed bags. They developed so much mould during the sea journey that it had to be removed with a vacuum cleaner!
- Protect outer containers, if necessary. Cardboard cartons are vulnerable to moisture. So are hessian sacks, which might be used for products that are not fragile. A plastic wrapping will usually offer adequate protection. Wooden boxes can easily absorb moisture and should be lined with plastic inside.

Protection against pilferage or loss

Outer containers must also serve the purpose of protection as far as possible against pilferage. If theft is undertaken on an organised basis, it is difficult to guard against it. Pilferers may have all the equipment necessary to undo containers and reseal them without leaving evidence. What you can protect yourself against to some extent is petty pilferage, by sealing boxes properly. Wrapping and sealing sacks also assists in this respect.

It is a good idea to band cartons, using a banding machine. This offers protection against their coming apart in transit. It also ensures the carton is packed tight, assisting protection against breakage.

Loss in transit is a considerable irritant in relationships between exporters and importers. If there is no evidence of tampering with the container, then each party is likely to think that the other is being at best inefficient in its counting when packing or unpacking, or at worst dishonest.

Economic handling by the importer

Packing and unpacking consignments is labour-intensive. In the countries which import most handicrafts, labour costs are high. Any additional work which has to be done will add to the cost of the product to the importer. It is important, therefore, to do whatever possible to simplify the job of the unpackers. If a product has more than one part, these should always be packed together. For example, Oxfam Trading received drums from Africa. They were individually wrapped, but the sticks were packed separately in another carton. We had to unwrap every one, put the sticks with it, and wrap it again. This process added about 5 per cent to the cost of the product. We would have rather paid a 5 per cent higher price to the producer to pack it properly.

Sometimes ease of handling is in conflict with economic transportation. Exporters might save space, and therefore cost, by packing different products inside one another. This takes more time to unpack in the importer's warehouse, but is obviously sensible.

The choice of outer container should be related to the products inside. Obviously, the first consideration is protection; the second is cost. The lighter the material used, the cheaper will be the freight cost if the consignment is sent by air. An importer would not appreciate wasting money by receiving textiles, for example, by air freight, in a wooden box. The third consideration is ease of handling. Heavy products should not be packed in large units, because they will become too heavy for people to handle. This can be a problem even in fully mechanised warehouses. At some stage in the handling process, people might need to pick up a box. It is generally better to use outer containers of a small size. Some exporters send consignments in baskets, made by local basket weavers. This is a good idea, if they offer adequate protection. The importer can sell the basket as well. Cardboard cartons can be re-used by importers for their own distribution. Wooden boxes are usually broken up, because they do not have scrap value. This might surprise some exporters, given that the boxes are quite expensive to make.

Safe receipt at destination

If a consignment is being sent on its own in a container, then the individual boxes do not need any marks. If it is being sent by freight or post, then each package must be marked. The way in which consignments are identified in international freight is a system of **shipping marks**. The exporter puts a design on to the packages — such as a quadrangle, a triangle with a dot inside, a circle with a line through it. The same design is reproduced on the invoice and transportation document. It is not actually necessary to put the exporter's name and address on the packages. In practice, most handicraft exporters do so, for a feeling of greater security. (The system of shipping marks does not apply to parcel post.) Each package must also be numbered, and also indicate the total number of packages in the consignment. This can be done by writing, for example, either 'no. 3 of 10' or, more simply '3/10'. Both the customs of the importing country and the importer require this information in order to be sure that parts of a consignment have not become separated.

If the customer has asked for any other marking, be sure to put it on. Oxfam Trading always requests that our code number, and the quantity of that product inside the package, be included. This assists our warehouse procedures. **Do not mark what the actual product is**. That could encourage pilferage. Nor should you put any information on labels which may become detached in transit.

There is a series of international symbols which give instructions about the handling of the packages. These may not necessarily be respected by the handlers of course! However it is worth knowing three, perhaps:

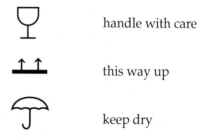

handle with care

this way up

keep dry

Handicrafts are extremely variable in size and shape, and often will not fit boxes which are available in standard sizes. There can even be variations in size of the individual items, especially if made by different producers, as usually happens. Quantities are often too small to bear the cost of having boxes made especially to measure. If a customer needs this, it should be investigated, because possibly it would cost even more to make in the importing country. There is often a scarcity of good packing materials, especially in the rural areas of producing countries. Even if the odds are against you, do not risk damaging your product or upsetting your customer by inadequate attention to the packing.

Summary

1 An export order contains eight main features: the product, labels and packaging, price, quantity, payment terms, delivery date, method of shipment and documentation required. All these details must be complied with in order to fulfil the order to the customer's specification. There are several possibilities for misunderstanding, often due to lack of complete clarity in the words used by the importer on the order form. Exporters sometimes cannot comply with one or more of the requirements, or may wish to suggest changes favourable to the importer. In all cases, it is important to discuss the situation with

the customer before proceeding to produce and despatch. All orders should be confirmed by the exporter to the importer.

2 Regular communication with customers will give you the best chance of obtaining further orders. Inform yourself about the timetables and procedures according to which your customers make decisions, so that you may have your offer in front of them at the right time. If you do not have your own fax machine, it is advisable to get access to a reliable fax service. Communication breeds confidence in relationships; lack of communication removes it.

3 Packing must be undertaken with great care, in order to transport a consignment safely and economically to your customer. Protection must be given against breakage, pilferage, and damage caused by changes in climate. Many common problems are avoidable by taking simple precautions, such as packing tightly to avoid movement inside boxes, and punching holes in plastic bags to allow ventilation. Pack with consideration for the cost of transportation, and the handling of the boxes by the importer. There is a system of marking packages and export invoices in order to identify international cargo.

9 DESPATCHING EXPORT CONSIGNMENTS

9.1 Exporting and importing formalities

In order to protect the interests of both exporter and importer, and also to fulfil legal requirements in the exporting and importing countries, certain procedures and controls regulate international trade.

The interests of the various parties are:

Exporter: to ensure that the consignment reaches the importer safely and promptly; to get paid.

Exporting country's government: to ensure that goods exported may legally be sent out of the country and are of exportable quality; that there is no mis-statement of value for the purpose of avoiding price controls or currency regulations; perhaps to raise revenues through export taxes; to record export data.

Importing country's government: to ensure that goods imported may legally enter the country and that they comply with import controls and quality standards; to raise revenues through duties or taxes; to record import data.

Importer: to receive the consignment safely and promptly.

The government authority responsible for monitoring and controlling trade is the customs. Export consignments must pass through the customs of their country, where they are liable to be inspected. In some countries consignments must also pass through other government departments, who have responsibility to control certain types of exports. For example, antiques or works of art might be restricted or liable to tax. There are no restrictions anywhere on the export of new handicrafts — unless they are made of a prohibited material, such as ivory; but several countries levy taxes on handicraft exports.

When the consignment reaches the importer's country, it is similarly liable to inspection by the customs authorities. It must be cleared by them before it can be received by the importer. Between the two customs authorities the consignment is carried by a transportation company, by road or sea or air. For reasons of security it will need insurance.

The physical movement and governmental control of goods in international trade is based on the completion and transfer of certain essential documents. They are:

Invoice: This is the document of sale, which provides the specification of goods. It is raised by the exporter, and is required by all parties.

Packing list: This provides details of which products are contained in which package. It is raised by the exporter, and is required by the customs of the importing country.

Transportation document: This is a receipt of the road transporter or postal authority; or airway bill or bill of lading. It is raised by the transportation company as a receipt for the consignment, and an undertaking to deliver it in the same condition as received. A bill of lading acts additionally as a document of title to the goods, and as such is required by the importer.

Certificate of origin: This is a document which is combined with a certificate of preferential trade agreement. There are two forms: the combined Generalised System of Preferences (GSP) (see Chapter 5.1) and Certificate of Origin Form A; and the EUR.1 Movement Certificate, within the Lome´ Convention. Either form is authorised by the government of the exporting country, and required by customs in the importing country in order to assess, together with the product type, liability for — or exemption from — duties.

Certificate of insurance: This is not always applicable. Many times exporters or importers have open cover policies which last for a fixed period — usually a year — so that an insurance certificate is not raised separately for each shipment.

Special import documents: For the movement of certain types of goods to certain countries, further documents must be supplied by the

<table>
<tr><td>

1. Goods consigned from (Exporter's business name, address, country)

PROYECTO EDUCATIVO PRODUCTIVO PARA LA
COMERCIALIZACION DEL ARTE TEXTIL.-
AV. SIMEON CAÑAS 8-35 ZONA 2
GUATEMALA, CITY GUATEMALA.

</td><td>

Reference No

002736

GENERALISED SYSTEM OF PREFERENCES

CERTIFICATE OF ORIGIN
(Combined declaration and certificate)

FORM A

Issued in GUATEMALA, CENTRAL AMERICA.
(country)

See Notes overleaf

</td></tr>
<tr><td>

2. Goods consigned to (Consignee's name, address, country)

OXFAM TRADING
MURDOCK ROAD, BICESTER
OXON OX6 7RF
GREAT BRITAIN.

</td><td></td></tr>
</table>

3. Means of transport and route (as far as known)

AIR FREIGHT
FROM:AIRPORT LA AURORA
GUATEMALA.
TO: AIRPORT OF ROTHERDAM
GREAT BRITAIN.

4. For official use

5. Item number	6. Marks and numbers of packages	7. Number and kind of packages; description of goods	8. Origin criterion (see Notes overleaf)	9. Gross weight or other quantity	10. Number and date of invoices
	518250386	3 BOXES CONTAINING: 7 TYPICAL BELTS, 5 TYPICAL TABLE CLOTH, 1 SET TYPICAL HATS, 10 TYPICAL BAGS, 2 TYPICAL TIGHT, 5 TYPICAL VEST, 1 TYPICAL BLANKET,4 TYPICAL RUG, 4 GLASES, 1 TYPICAL JACKETS, 6 TYPICAL SHIRTS, ALL 100% COTTON HAND MADE IN GUATEMALA WITH FIRST QUALITY MATERIALS.-	"P"	32.5kg	MAY-02-91 00018

11. Certification

It is hereby certified, on the basis of control carried out, that the declaration by the exporter is correct.

LIC. CARLOS SANTIZO GIL
JEFE ... VENTANILLA UNICA
Guatemala **3 MAY 1991**
Place and date signature and stamp of certifying authority

12. Declaration by the exporter

The undersigned hereby declares that the above details and statements are correct; that all the goods were produced in

GUATEMALA, CENTRAL AMERICA.
(country)

and that they comply with the origin requirements specified for those goods in the Generalised System of Preferences for goods exported to

GREAT BRITAIN.
(importing country)

GUATEMALA MAY 03, 1,991.-
Place and date signature of authorised signatory

PROYECTO EDUCATIVO - PRODUCTIVO

Fig 22: *Combined GSP and Certificate of Origin*

MOVEMENT CERTIFICATE

1. Exporter (Name, full address, country) USHINDI YOUTH PROJECT P.O. BOX 50504, NAIROBI	**EUR. 1 A** 321181 *See* notes overleaf before completing this form

2. Application for a certificate to be used in preferential trade between

E E C

and

A C P

(insert appropriate countries, groups of countries or territories)

3. Consignee (Name, full address, country) (Optional)
OXFAM TRADING
MURDOCK ROAD, BICESTER
OXON, OX6 7RF
BRITAIN

4. Country, group of countries or territory in which the products are considered as originating KENYA	**5.** Country, group of countries or territory of destination ENGLAND

6. Transport details (Optional)

PARCEL POST

7. Remarks

*If goods are not packed, indicate number of articles or state "in bulk" as appropriate	**8. Item number; marks and numbers/Number and kind of packages*; description of goods**

8. description of goods	**9. Gross weight (kg.) or other measure (litres, cu. m., etc.)**	**10. Invoices** (Optional)
TWO PARCEL, ADD , 2400 BATIK CARDS HAND MADE, MADE OF CLOTHS, DYES AND PAPER	30Kg	

KENYA EXTERNAL TRADE AUTHORITY
P.O. Box 43137 NAIROBI

13/3/81

11. CUSTOMS ENDORSEMENT Stamp Declaration certified. Export document† Form .... No. .... Customs Office: .... Issuing country or territory: .... Date.. .... (Signature)	**12. DECLARATION BY THE EXPORTER** I, the undersigned, declare that the goods described above meet the conditions required for the issue of this certificate. NAIROBI 12/3/86 Place and date:....................................... USHINDI YOUTH PROJECT P.O BOX 50504 NAIROBI (Signature)

†Complete only where the regulations of the exporting country or territory require.

Fig.23: *EUR.1 Movement Certificate*

exporting country in order to fulfil customs requirements of the importing country, or perhaps to enable the importer to obtain preferential treatment in respect of duties. For example, health certificates are required by some countries. A handloom certificate would enable an importer to obtain exemption from duty on hand-woven textiles.

Special export licences: Some goods are covered by international agreements, such as the Multi-Fibre Arrangement. These may be traded internationally only under licence. The exporter must procure an export licence and send this to the importer for procurement of an import licence.

The above documents pass from the exporting to the importing country. **Only originals, not copies, of certification documents are acceptable.** In addition there is a separate series of procedures and documents between the exporter and its government, and between the importer and its government. In other words, the exporter has to get authorisation for the despatch, and the importer for the receipt. Exact procedures vary from country to country. In most cases, it will be necessary for an exporter to be registered. In some countries, this is sufficient to be able to make an export shipment. In others, it will be necessary to apply for a licence on each occasion.

The main responsibility of the importer is to make the declaration to the customs of the type of goods being imported. Importation works on a system of **product classification**. Each product type, as established by the Customs Co-operation Council, carries a customs classification code. When an invoice is submitted to the importing country's customs, each product must bear a customs classification number. This is the basis for determining whether the products may enter freely or not, and whether or not they are liable to duty.

The majority of handicrafts enter freely into most countries. Certain products will be allowed into a country only if the importer obtains a licence. Others will be passed by customs only on payment of the applicable rate of duty. Duty is always paid on the invoice value plus the cost of freight and insurance, in other words the value at which the goods land in the country of importation.

It is the responsibility of the importer to present all the necessary documents to the customs, and request them to clear the goods. Until that is done, the consignment will remain in the customs shed. Figure 24 shows the documents required to send a consignment of handwoven cushion covers from India to Britain by sea freight:

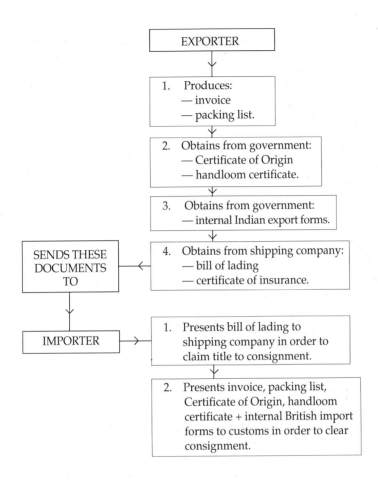

Fig. 24: *Documents required in the export of handicrafts*

Not surprisingly, there is quite a lot of paperwork involved in international trade. It would take an enormous amount of time for exporters and importers to obtain and present all the necessary documents for each shipment. If they were not located in their capital cities it would be almost impossible. This is why each of them normally employs an agent in order to process all the documentary requirements. Oxfam Trading imports all its consignments by using an agent, except the ones which arrive by parcel post. Agencies are specialist companies who obtain the documents and liaise with the customs authorities.

Export agents will normally also offer to arrange the international transportation. This can be a valuable service, as they often have good contacts with the various companies and can negotiate favourable rates. Those who do this are known as clearing and forwarding agents — or freight forwarders — because they clear the consignment through customs, and forward it to the importer. **The services of the agent will be billed to the exporter.** If the exporter has sold to the importer on an FOB basis, then those costs are the exporter's responsibility. If, however, it is an ex works contract, then the exporter may subsequently invoice the importer for the same amount. Import agents offer the additional service of making payments on the importer's behalf. If the freight bill is being paid by the importer, which is a common arrangement, then in practice the importer's agent will pay it to the transportation company, and subsequently pass the bill on to the importer.

By using an agent, exporting becomes a great deal simpler. The exporter must prepare the invoice and the packing list, but the rest can be passed over. In summary, the process is not so forbidding:

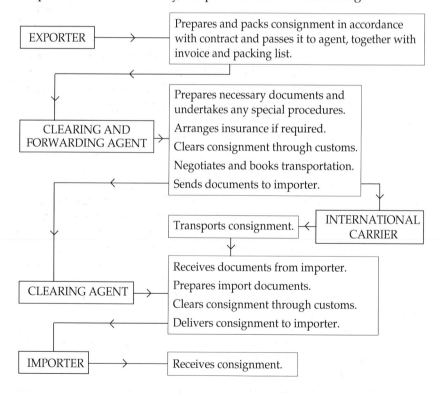

Fig. 25: *Using agents for exporting*

Of course, the services of agents have to be paid for. Some exporters use them only to clear a consignment through customs, preferring to manage the documentation and negotiating of shipping for themselves. In this case, it is their responsibility to forward the documents to the customer. **Any small handicraft business can undertake an export**. All it has to do is:

- Register for export with its government, if this is required.
- Find a reliable agent. Inevitably, some agents are more efficient and cheaper than others. The agent will confirm all the procedures required.

Because the importer may clear the goods only by presenting the documents to the customs, **it is essential that these arrive either before, or together with, the consignment**. If the goods arrive without documents, they are stored pending presentation of these. For this service, transportation companies levy a daily charge — known as demurrage — which varies according to the size of the consignment. Regrettably, this happens quite often in Oxfam Trading's experience.

If a consignment is sent by sea, there is usually plenty of time for the exporter (or agent) to forward the documents to the importer in the post. If it is sent by air, then there is not. The best procedure in that case is for the exporter to **send the documents together with the consignment**. They can travel in a waterproof envelope attached to one of the packets. On arrival, the importer's agent will collect them, prepare the other importing documents required, and clear the consignment. An alternative is to send the documents by courier. This would be necessary if, for some reason, the documents are not ready to accompany the consignment, or not allowed to do so by the exporting country, which is sometimes the case. The important thing from the importer's point of view is that there is **no delay between the receipt of the consignment and the receipt of the documents**, for each day costs money in the form of demurrage charges as well as possibly causing the loss of sales. Before forwarding the documents, the exporter will need to have a secure agreement with the importer about payment for the goods.

The importer's agent must be advised about the arrival of a consignment. There is a section in the transportation document with an instruction to 'Notify Party'. The exporter — or agent — will inform the transporter of the name, address, and telephone number of the importer's agent. It might also be marked on the actual packets, if it is not a containerised consignment. When a consignment arrives, the transporter will notify the agent. This means that the importer must ensure that the exporter is sent details of its agent, so that this information can be passed to the transporter. Oxfam Trading sends out with orders a 'guide for exporters' which includes details of our agents (we use two) as well as our bank, and general instructions about fulfilment of the order. This shortens the procedure by which the transporter would otherwise have to notify the importer who then instructs the agent. The importer must forward to its agent without delay the documents sent by the exporter.

Consignments sent by parcel post undergo a simpler procedure. Agents are not normally involved. An exporter may deposit the parcel directly at a post office, together with a description of the contents. It will be cleared by the post offices of the exporting and importing countries through their customs, and delivered to the importer. The exporter has the same responsibility to send appropriate documents to the importer: an invoice, certificate of origin and transportation document (postal receipt), plus a packing list if there is more than one parcel.

Some small handicraft businesses are under the misunderstanding that post parcel packages may be sent overseas without documents. This is not the case. The only time it is ever possible is when sending a very small consignment of samples, by marking the parcel 'Samples. No Commercial Value'. This is because any duty payable on just a few items would be so small that customs would not consider it worth the cost of collection. So they would usually let a small parcel of samples through without the import papers required in all other cases.

Preparation of the invoice should not be difficult, even for an inexperienced exporter. An invoice must contain:

- a full description of the goods;
- the shipping marks (i.e. what is written on the packets);
- the price of the goods;
- the terms of the contract (e.g FOB Mbabane);
- details of any freight and insurance costs payable;
- details of any special licences or forms required.

It is very important indeed that the invoice is correct and complete. Remember that it is the importer's responsibility to present documents to the customs. **If customs decide to open a consignment and find items incorrectly described or not included, they invariably treat this as a serious matter**. The importer can be prosecuted. Customs generally operate a system of random checks. This is why they insist

HANDICRAFT CO-OPERATIVE EXPORT LTD.
(HANDCOOPEX)
P.O.BOX 385
MBABANE
SWAZILAND

Telephone and Fax: 48326   Telex: 2413

INVOICE NO: EX/72/91

To: ABC Import Ltd.
    1 Snow Lane
    London EC1X 2CY

Purchase Order No. A5200

Country of Origin: Swaziland

Country of Destination: U.K.

Notify Party/Address:

Smith Clearing Ltd.
Freight House
Bell Wharf
Manchester   M6 2EG

Terms of Delivery & Payment:
FOB Mbabane. Cash
                against documents

Vessel: African Queen

AWB/B/L No: MB 64251 - 4

PRODUCT CODE NO.	QUANTITY	ARTICLE	UNIT PRICE US$	TOTAL PRICE US$
SW 6834	149	Round basket, 10"	5.25	782.25
SW 6835	100	Nesting S/2 baskets	8.50	850.00
SW 6839	145	Oblong basket, 10"	6.00	870.00
SW 4160	30	Royal Swazi necklace	8.50	255.00
SW 4161	50	Royal Swazi bracelet	4.50	225.00
SW 4167	50	Royal Swazi earring	3.50	175.00

TOTAL FOB MBABANE US$ 3157.25

SHIPPING MARKS

TOTAL NO. OF PACKAGES

....
Authorised Signature

Fig 26: *Invoice*

157

HANDICRAFT CO-OPERATIVE EXPORT LTD.
(HANDCOOPEX)
P.O.BOX 385
MBABANE
SWAZILAND

Telephone and Fax: 48326   Telex: 2413

PACKING LIST

INVOICE NO: EX/72/91

VESSEL: AFRICAN QUEEN

AWB/B/L NO: MB 64251-4

TOTAL NO. OF PACKAGES: 3

SHIPPING MARKS:

BOX NO. 1	SW 6834 SW 6835	149 Round basket 30 Nesting S/2 baskets
BOX NO. 2	SW 6835 SW 6839	30 nesting S/2 baskets 145 oblong basket, 10"
BOX NO. 3	SW 6835 SW 4160 SW 4161 SW 4162	40 nesting S/2 baskets 30 Royal Swazi necklace 50 Royal Swazi bracelet 50 Royal Swazi earring

Fig 27: *Packing list*

on receiving a packing list, so they can spot-check any part of a consignment. They will also test any suspicious product for conformity with safety standards, and refuse it entry if it does not meet the required standard.

Demurrage is also charged while customs inspect an importer's goods. We once paid over $400 demurrage charge on a container from Thailand which customs decided to search. They found a discrepancy between the invoice and the contents, because the supplier had omitted to list a sample, which was being sent free of charge. They refused to release the container until we had obtained a new invoice from the supplier, which took us nearly three weeks (it was before the introduction of the fax machine). The sample turned out to be rather expensive!

Nothing must be omitted from the invoice. It is perfectly acceptable to include a few samples listed 'free of charge', but **they must always appear on the invoice**. If you are selling on an ex works basis, it is helpful to the importer to include the transportation and clearing charges on the same invoice if possible. It may not be possible if your clearing agent is slow in advising you of these, or if the consignment has to go by air freight and the documents leave immediately. In that case, you must send a separate invoice. You should not include requests for payments in a subsequent letter. Any claim for **payment must be made by a formal invoice**. The importer needs this for accounting purposes.

Before despatching a consignment, an exporter needs to be clear whose responsibility it is to insure it. It is a detail to be clarified if necessary at the time of confirming an order. If the exporter arranges insurance, this must be for at least the invoiced value of the goods. The risks to be covered must include the transport of the goods from the warehouse to the port or airport, storage while awaiting loading, actual transportation, offloading and storage on arrival, and final transport to the importer's warehouse.

9.2 International transportation

There are four main methods of international transportation: air freight, sea freight, air parcel post, and sea parcel post. Each has advantages and disadvantages.

Sea freight

This is the most common method used in the international handicraft trade. The cost of the ocean journey is almost always cheaper than the equivalent journey by air freight. A consignment sent by sea is charged **according to its volume**, or measurement. There might be a minimum charge, so that very small consignments would actually pay as much as larger ones. Increasingly, sea freight has become containerised. This means that a consignment is sent in a sealed metal container. If an exporter books a container, the same rate is paid whether it is filled or not. Containers have the advantages of offering better protection against pilferage or loss, requiring the contents to be less extensively packed, and charging less per cubic metre than general cargo. A great deal of Oxfam Trading's imports are containerised. The method also makes unpacking easier in our warehouse. There are two sizes of container: 20 feet long (26 cubic metres volume) and 40 feet long (55 cubic metres).

Nevertheless, sea freight has certain disadvantages. Consider these comments from our supplier in Cameroon:

> 'Quite a good number of our big partners in USA and Europe are now turning to sea freight. Of course, this can be understood because the lower the landing charges, the better the chances are of selling our products. We can already see that shipping light items like baskets, calabash rattles, etc. by sea can equally be expensive. Sea-worthy cases are expensive to make. The shipping agents are not flexible. The processing of documents for sea freight is slow and time consuming. Several trips have to be made to Douala, the sea port, before a consignment leaves the port. Charges from forwarding companies are equally high. Quite some money has to be invested in wooden cases. This ties up capital. Sea freight and other handling charges must be paid to the agent before the consignment is taken on board. This situation needs an increase in working capital. It takes quite some time for a customer to get his consignment by sea before making arrangements to send us money. How cost effective is this method?'[19]

Cameroon is a country with a sea port. Clearly the situation is worse for a landlocked country, from which freight must travel a long way by road to the port of another country. In some countries, this is logistically so difficult that sea freight is not a viable option.

These additional packing and internal transport costs may make sea freight less competitive than air freight. Where an exporter is situated closer to the international airport than the port, then even within the same country, **the relative cost needs to be looked at carefully**. For example, Oxfam Trading imports a number of products by air freight from Kenya. This is because the air freight rates from Nairobi to London are quite low, and packing and internal transport costs for despatch from the capital to the seaport of Mombasa quite high. However, in general, more than three-quarters of our freight arrives by sea, and we save several thousand pounds each month by using sea rather than air. Of course, sea freight is slower than air freight. Sometimes it is important to receive a consignment quickly, even if this will incur a higher freight cost. **But it is the importer who must decide**. For example, an importer would be annoyed to receive a consignment by air freight two months earlier than the delivery date, when it could have been sent more cheaply by sea freight. As always, the exporter must follow the customer's instructions on the order, unless there is a good reason to suggest a change.

Sea freight was, of course, in existence for centuries before the invention of the aeroplane. The system of documentation employed today in sea freight is based on traditional methods. The bill of lading was formerly kept by the ship's captain, who was responsible to the exporter for collecting payment from the importer. Only when payment was made did the captain release the cargo. In exactly the same way today, the bill of lading acts as a deed of title to the goods. Without the original copy of it, the importer cannot receive the consignment. The difference between tradition and modern practice is that payments are now handled by banks, not shipping lines, and that the original bill of lading is given to the exporter when the shipping line issues it. It is now the exporter's responsibility to ensure that it is forwarded to the importer in good time for the arrival of the ship.

The cost of sea freight varies among shipping lines. Many of them belong to an association known as Conference, and charge the same rate per volume. Even so, because of frequency of sailings, or amount of cargo, some Conference lines can offer a better rate on some routes by consolidating different consignments into containers. The cost of containers on the same route can be different among different companies. There are shipping lines who are not members of Conference, and who tend to undercut the rates. It is important to consider not just rates but also service. Exporters and importers need reliable shipping lines, who offer frequent sailings, and comply with their timetables. Conference lines publish schedules which enable exporters to plan despatches. An exporter or its freight forwarder has to keep in touch with the different lines to be sure that it is up to date with the best service for any particular destination.

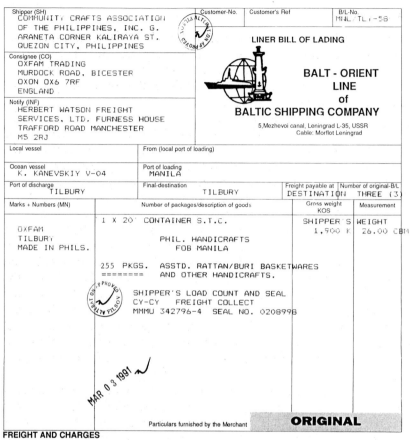

Fig. 28: *A bill of lading*

Air freight

The airway bill is not as important as the bill of lading. It does not act as a deed of title to a consignment. An importer does not need the original copy in order to be able to claim the goods. But at least one copy is required as a record of the details of the consignment and the charges made for transporting it.

Unless a contract is made whereby the exporter is responsible for the freight cost, such as CIF, then the cost of international transport is the importer's responsibility. However, it is the exporter who arranges the actual despatch. A curious and potentially difficult situation results, in which the party which negotiates the rates does not actually pay the bills. The first information the importer will have about the freight rate is on the bill of lading or airway bill. The rates for air freight are generally more variable than those for sea freight. There are more opportunities for getting special rates. It is therefore especially important that these are **carefully investigated and negotiated**. Oxfam Trading has often paid a certain rate, only to find when visiting the exporting country that a better rate was available. It cannot be assumed that an agent will automatically locate the best rate, although a good one will. An exporter needs to make its agent aware that it, too, is keeping a check on rates charged by other agents. The threat of competition for business is always a good motivator for more efficient performance.

As with shipping lines, airlines have an association, the International Air Transport Association (IATA). This has standard cargo rates. Air freight is charged according to weight, unlike sea freight. The higher the weight, the lower the rate per kilogram. The highest rate is charged for consignments less than 45 kg. There is a second rate for weights between 45 kg and 100 kg, a third for 100 kg - 500 kg, and a fourth for more than half a ton. The rates vary according to destination, of course. However, as in sea freight, the rate might be the same over quite a large range of destinations, for example, all western Europe.

The scope for reductions from the standard rates come in four ways. First, as in sea freight, certain airlines can consolidate cargo on some busy routes and offer more favourable rates. Second, just as there are non-Conference shipping lines, so some airlines do not belong to IATA and can offer cheaper rates. Third, and most importantly, there is a system of commodity rates in airfreight. These are special rates negotiated by governments for exports of particular importance. These can often include handicrafts, or at least certain types of handicrafts. Finally, there are, in addition to scheduled services, chartered cargo flights. These are flights booked by companies especially for the

055 | 5633 7735   055- 5633 7735

Shipper's Name and Address	Shipper's account Number	Not negotiable

Shipper's Name and Address: ALI BROTHERS, HASSANABAD, RAINAWARI, SRINAGAR/KASHMIR.

Air Waybill
Issued by
Alitalia CARGO SYSTEM
ALITALIA.S.p.A. P.le Giulio Pastore, 6 ROMA
CAP. SOC. LIT. 975 MILIARDI INT. VERSATO
C. F. 00476680582 · P. IVA 00903301000
R. T. N. 2029/46 · C.C.I.A.A. N. 135156   Member of International Air Transport Association

Copies 1, 2 and 3 of this Air Waybill are originals and have the same validity.

Consignee's Name and Address:
NATIONAL WESTMINSTER BANK PLC,
NATIONAL WESTMINSTEE HOUSE, THE
GROVE SLOUGHT BERKS.SLI IQB U.K.

It is agreed that the goods described herein are accepted in apparent good order and condition (except as noted) for carriage SUBJECT TO THE CONDITIONS OF CONTRACT ON THE REVERSE HEREOF. THE SHIPPER'S ATTENTION IS DRAWN TO THE NOTICE CONCERNING CARRIERS' LIMITATION OF LIABILITY. Shipper may increase such limitation of liability by declaring a higher value for carriage and paying a supplemental charge if required.
Le merci qui descritte sono accettate in apparente buono stato e condizione (eccezione fatta per i casi in cui è dichiarato altrimenti) per il trasporto in conformità alle CONDIZIONI CONTRATTUALI DESCRITTE SUL RETRO. SI RICHIAMA L'ATTENZIONE DEL MITTENTE SULL'AVVISO CONCERNENTE LA LIMITAZIONE DI RESPONSABILITA DEL VETTORE. Il mittente può aumentare il limite di responsabilità del vettore dichiarando un valore più elevato per il trasporto e pagando, ove richiesto, una tariffa addizionale.

Issuing Carrier's Agent Name and City:
OMNI MARG TRAVELS PVT.LTD. JAIPUR

Accounting Information
FREIGHT TO PAY

Agent's IATA Code: 14-3-8335 3 | Account No.

Airport of Departure (Addr. of first Carrier) and requested Routing: NEW DELHI   AZ

Codice fiscale / Partita I.V.A. del Mittente | Imprenditore Non imprenditore ☐ PF ☐ SD

to	By First Carrier	Routing and Destination	to	by	to	by	Currency	WT/VAL PPD COLL	Other PPD COLL	Declared Value for Carriage	Declared Value for Customs
LON	AZ						INR	C	C	N V D	330456/-

Airport of Destination: L O N D O N (UK)

Amount of Insurance

INSURANCE - If Carrier offers insurance, and such insurance is requested in accordance with conditions on reverse hereof, indicate amount to be insured in figures in box marked "amount of insurance"
ASSICURAZIONE - Qualora il Vettore offra una assicurazione e tale assicurazione sia richiesta in base alle condizioni indicate a tergo, indicare l'importo da assicurare in cifre nella casella "importo assicurato"

Handling Information:
NOTIFY: OXFAM TRADING MURDOCK ROAD, BICKESTER, OXON OX6 7RF, BRITAIN.
TEL BICESTER (0869) 245011 TLX: 838930 OX BRIDG. ONE ENV. CONTD. DOCS. ATTD

(For U.S.A. only) These commodities licensed by USA for ultimate destination .... DIVERSION CONTRARY TO USA LAW PROHIBITED

No of Pieces RCP	Gross Weight	Kg lb	Rate Class / Commodity item No	Chargeable Weight	Rate / Charge	Total	Nature and Quantity of Goods (incl. Dimensions or Volume)
34	819	KC	9525	819kg	41-25	33783-75	SAID TO CONTAIN HAND MADE ARTISTIC PAPIER PACHIE ARTICLES S.B:NO: GR.NO: GP: 160375 RBI DA: 00210 IEC:1888004002

Prepaid	Weight Charge	Collect	Other Charges	P.B.A. Fee
	33784-00		AWA:30-00 LCL:FRT:2291/-	

Valuation Charge
IAAI.CH:328/-   CTG:300-00   CCF:750-00

Insurance Premium

Tax
DBC: 370-00

Total other Charges Due Agent: 3699

Shipper certifies that the particulars on the face hereof are correct and that insofar as any part of the consignment contains dangerous goods, such part is properly described by name and is in proper condition for carriage by air according to the applicable Dangerous Goods Regulations.
Il mittente dichiara che le indicazioni contenute sul fronte della LTA sono esatte, e che qualora una parte della spedizione contenga merci pericolose, tale parte è debitamente indicata ed è nelle condizioni richieste ai fini del trasporto per via aerea secondo le norme sulle Merci Pericolose.

Total other Charges Due Carrier: 370-00

L.C.CHAMANLAL & COMPANY
Signature of Shipper or his Agent

Total prepaid	Total collect

(9th May'91)
9th May'91
Executed on (Date) at (Place)
Signature of Issuing Carrier or its Agent

055- 5633 7735

I.V.A. non imponibile Art. 9/1° C. DPR 633/72 Pro quota

---- ORIGINAL 3 (FOR SHIPPER)

Fig. 29: *An airway bill*

transportation of goods, because it might be more efficient for them to do this than to send the goods on scheduled services. Sometimes additional space can be available on such flights, at low cost, for handicrafts.

Although air freight rates are levied according to weight, there are maximum volumes that are accepted against these weights. If the volume is greater, then a volumetric surcharge is added. For example, a consignment of large bulky baskets weighing just 50kg might be charged as if they weighed twice that amount. This surcharge would not always apply on charter air freight.

Handicraft consignments which are not volumetrically large, and which can obtain a favourable rate, perhaps a commodity rate, can often be sent economically by air freight. There are other advantages. As the supplier in Cameroon points out, the payment should be made more quickly; although that depends on the method of payment agreed. There is not normally a need to pack as protectively. For example, a manufacturer of ceramics in Peru charged 10 per cent on top of the ex works price for air freight packing, and 20 per cent for sea freight packing. An exporter should try to make available an economic air freight option if at all possible. There may be times when an importer needs the speed it offers, without wanting the penalty of removing the profit from the consignment because of high freight costs.

Parcel post

When a consignment is sent by air or sea post, the formalities are simpler. Only small packages may be sent by post. There are limitations in two respects:

Weight: parcels may not exceed a certain weight. This is normally 10 kg for air post, 20 kg for sea post; but it might be different in certain countries. If a consignment is heavier, it must be split up into different parcels.

Size: there is usually a restriction on both length and length plus girth for any parcel. These are measured as shown in Figure 30.

Parcels for export are despatched at main post offices. They must be marked with the importer's name and address, and also the exporter's. If there is more than one parcel in the same consignment, it must be marked accordingly. The exporter will be required to make a declaration of contents and value. Parcels are subject to random

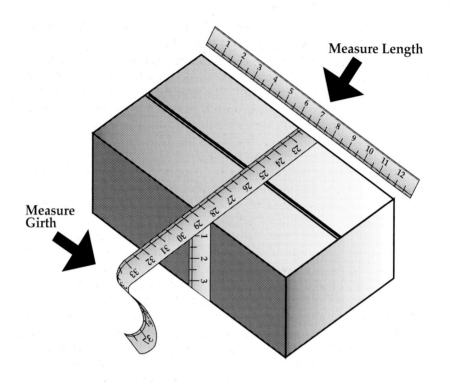

Measure Length

Measure Girth

Addressing the parcel:

(pencil not acceptable)

From:
Name
Address
City   Country

To:

Carton

[ ] of [ ]

Name
Address
City
Country

Fig. 30: *Measuring and addressing a parcel for export*

166

inspection by customs. In a number of countries, a post office official inspects the contents before sealing the parcel.

Parcels may be sent by sea or air. The former is considerably cheaper, but the slowest of all the freight methods. Air parcel post is usually quick. It is a convenient method for importers to receive a small consignment. However, it is much less convenient for larger consignments, broken up into several parcels. These can often get separated in transit. Also, it is expensive. The rate per kilogram is invariably higher than that for air freight.

Small consignments can usually be transported more cheaply by post than by freight. Even if the postage cost itself appears higher, the overall cost would be lower because it does not incur customs and agency charges. However, the larger the consignment, the less those charges are relative to the invoice value and the more important is the actual rate for transporting the goods. So larger consignments may be less economical by post. Parcel post is also less secure. In some countries, the postal system is so bad that exporters simply will not use it.

Unlike freight, parcels cannot be sent on the basis that the importer pays the postage. This must be paid at the time the exporter hands over the parcel. If a consignment is being sent on an ex works or FOB basis, the charge for the postage should simply be added to the invoice, or invoiced separately. Figure 31 illustrates the costs of the various options, in an example produced by the Kenyan government.[20]

Estimated comparative cost (Kenyan shillings) of shipping a mixed order of handicrafts from Nairobi to New York
(Mixed goods are wood carvings, Kisii stone items, leather items and sisal baskets)

Gross Weight of order	Air Parcel Post	Sea Parcel Post	Air Freight	Sea Freight
1	2	2	3	4
20kg	785.5	205.0	1096.0	2595.0
100kg	3927.5	1025.0	2390.0	2595.0
450kg	17673.0	4612.5	8800.0	2595.0
1000kg	-	-	17600.0	2595.0

Notes:
1 Does not include packing costs.
2 Order is divided into separate parcels, none exceeding 10kg.
3 Cost of air freight only: does not include agency fees or local transport charges.
4 Based on 1000kg/cubic metre crate with handling charges between Nairobi and Mombasa.
(Insurance not included in calculations.)

Fig. 31: *Comparative cost of options for international freight*

Two points emerge clearly:

- for larger consignments, air parcel post is not economical;
- sea freight becomes more advantageous as the consignment gets larger, but for smaller consignments air freight or air parcel post is cheaper.

These conclusions would be generally valid for most international freight. However, the circumstances will be different in particular countries. In the interests of offering the most efficient and cost-effective service to your customer, you must take the trouble to **research the freight options**. The price which the importer works with is the price into its warehouse. Freight and clearing charges are part of the buying price. If these costs can be reduced, the importer can sell more profitably, or reduce its own selling price. Either way, the possibility of the exporter receiving more orders is improved.

9.3　Methods of payment

Receiving payment fully and promptly is the final objective of all the effort that has been made to obtain and supply an export order. It is not only the exporter who has an interest in it. Governments, too, require evidence that export consignments have been paid for and that payment has been made in foreign currency. The significance of foreign currency is that it can be converted internationally for the payment of imports. The currencies of most countries which produce handicrafts cannot be; they are what is called 'non-convertible' currencies. The government of the exporting country, through its national bank, converts the receipt from the overseas customer into local currency, which is what the exporter receives. In some countries exporters are allowed to keep a certain proportion of the payment in the currency in which the importer has made the payments. This is usually either to enable them to buy imported components of their export product, or to allow them to convert a percentage of the payment at a higher rate than the official one. Governments sometimes allow this in order to assist exporters in periods of high inflation when the official and street values of their currencies are widely different.

Failure to receive payment within the stipulated time — which varies from country to country — can cause considerable problems for an exporter, on whom the responsibility lies to collect it from the customer. Exporters can and do receive fines, or lose their export registration. This is all the more reason to establish a secure method of payment.

An exporter can consign goods and send the documents to the importer directly. This removes any form of guarantee that payment will be made. It is a system to be used **only with well-established customers in whom you have complete trust**; or, of course, if a full pre-payment has been made. It should never be used with new customers, and especially not in countries where you are not otherwise trading. Sadly, there are many small handicraft businesses which have had bad experiences after sending consignments overseas on misplaced trust without taking payment guarantees; sometimes they have never been paid. There is risk in all business. If you are going to seek new customers, you inevitably risk meeting a dishonest one. If an importer has your goods and will not pay, you are in an extremely weak negotiating position. Legal proceedings would probably be unrealistic. You cannot, on the other hand, ask all customers to pay fully in advance. You will not get many orders that way. So you need to take precautions.

There are two main ways of protecting yourself. One is to insist that, when the order is confirmed, the importer makes a **legally binding commitment to pay** at the time of shipment. This can be drawn up so that the exporter automatically obtains the payment from a bank on presentation of the export documents. This is the documentary credit (better known as letter of credit) system. The other method is to consign the documents or goods or both not to the importer, but to the importer's bank, under instruction that the goods be released only against payment or a binding promise to pay. This is the system of documentary collection. The first method is fairly safe for the exporter. The second one could fail if the importer goes out of business or refuses to accept the consignment. Both methods rely on the integrity of banks.

Documentary credit

The letter of credit system is 'a written undertaking given by a bank on behalf of the buyer to pay the seller an amount of money within a specific time, provided the seller presents documents strictly in accordance with the terms laid down in the Letter of Credit'.[21] On receipt of the order confirmation, the importer instructs its bank to open a credit for the required amount in favour of the exporter's bank. After shipment, the exporter presents all the documents to its bank, and provided the terms of the letter of credit have been adhered to, the bank pays immediately. The exporter, therefore, receives payment upon making shipment, irrespective of when the goods arrive with the importer. There can be further advantage to the exporter, in that in some countries credit facilities are made available at favourable rates of interest to exporters holding letters of credit.

A documentary credit can be revocable (which means that the importer can cancel or amend it at any time until the payment to the exporter has been effected), or irrevocable (which means that the exporter and importer must both agree to any amendment). It can also be confirmed (which means a guarantee is given to the exporter by its bank that payment will be made even if the importer's bank should fail to pay) or unconfirmed (in which there is no such guarantee). Hence, a confirmed, irrevocable letter of credit is a guaranteed system of payment. Many exporters insist on it for that reason.

Importers like it less. In the first place, it is an expensive means of payment. An administrative charge is made to set it up; and the importer has also to pay interest to the bank for the reserve on the bank's funds before payment. Second, there is more work and expense if the letter of credit has to be altered at any time. This is quite common, especially if an exporter is delivering late, as the letter of credit states a time limit. Oxfam Trading has had several experiences of needing to alter letters of credit to suppliers, sometimes just because a vessel did not sail on the due date, not through any fault of the exporter. While we always pay our suppliers by the method they prefer, we do not encourage them to choose the letter of credit system, which represents the lowest form of trust between seller and buyer.

Documentary collection

In this system the exporter similarly makes the claim for payment through its bank by presenting the documents to it after shipment. In this case, the credit has not already been set up by the importer, so that the exporter's bank does not make an immediate payment. Instead, it sends the documents to the importer's bank, which either makes the payment before releasing the documents to the importer, or releases them against a legally enforceable promise to pay.

When a documentary collection system is employed, the claim for payment is made on what is called a bill of exchange. The exporter, who raises this, may request immediate payment, or may alternatively agree to offer a period of credit to the customer. Immediately payment is claimed by a bill of exchange payable at sight. This system is commonly called 'cash against documents'. In this case, the importer's bank makes the payment before releasing the documents. Credit for a fixed period can be offered by a term bill of exchange, which defines a date in the future when payment is due. The importer is required in that case to sign an acceptance of the bill in order to obtain the documents. In this way, the provision of credit to an overseas customer does not necessarily entail risk of non-payment. The signed acceptance is legally enforceable in the courts of the importing country, and the bank will make the payment at the due date.

Documentary collection is an effective method of payment for consignments sent by sea freight. It suits the exporter because it offers the security of bank guarantees. Because the bill of lading gives legal title to the goods, the importer must either pay or promise to pay before the goods can be obtained. It suits the importer as well, because payment is made near the time of receiving the shipment.

The system is less suitable for other transportation methods. When a consignment is sent by air freight, the importer needs the documents very quickly, because the goods will arrive in a few days. If they are sent via the exporter's bank to the importer's bank, the delay may well lead to demurrage bills for the importer. If the exporter sends them directly to the importer, either attached to the consignment or separately by courier, then the importer will be happy, but the exporter loses any security that payment will be made. The way around this difficulty is to despatch the documents together with the goods, but to consign both goods and documents to the importer's bank, with a bill of exchange. There will be no delay in clearing the consignment, but the importer may obtain the documents to do this only on payment or promise to pay. Some countries will only permit exporters to despatch documents with the consignment if this system is being used. What happens is that, in effect, the despatch is delayed a few days in order to prepare the bill of exchange which accompanies the goods. A parcel sent by post can be consigned to the importer's bank in exactly the same way.

Payments in advance

It is common practice for Oxfam Trading's suppliers to request some proportion of the total payment in advance. This is not so much for reasons of security, but in order to obtain working capital. Money is needed to buy raw materials or pay wages during production of the order. If importers are willing to pay something in advance, then so much the better. The payment of the balance can still be claimed by documentary collection if required. If an advance has been paid, it is important to delete this amount from the final invoice.

Oxfam Trading offers to pay in advance for sample consignments from new contacts. It is cheaper and easier to do this than to administer documentary collection for very small amounts of money. If a potential new customer orders samples, it is reasonable for an exporter to request prepayment. For this purpose a proforma invoice needs to be sent, preferably adding the transportation cost.

Open account

This means trusting the customer! Goods and documents are consigned directly to the importer, and payment is awaited. Oxfam Trading conducts a lot of its business in this way. It is the method which suits us best, but we do not encourage exporters to use it for all their exports, for they might extend the trust unjustifiably to a less reputable importer.

With documentary credit or collection, money is transferred from the importer's bank to the exporter's. Advance or open account payments may also be handled in this way. It is by far the safest means of sending money overseas. Transfers may be effected by mail or by telex. The latter is quicker, and it is Oxfam Trading's normal method. In order to make transfers, an importer must, of course, have the full bank account details of the exporter. This information should be provided to any new customer at the time of confirming an order.

Banks have their own system of transferring money, through correspondent banks. The process can take a long time. We have received complaints from suppliers that payments have been delayed for several weeks after instructions have been given to our bank. It is a regular conversation topic between our payments office and our bank, but in practice we cannot control the route by which the money is transferred between banks.

Another method by which importers can pay exporters is by purchase of a draft. This is an international postal order in the currency of the exporter's invoice. It is only as reliable as the postal system. Drafts can get lost in the post, or even fall into the wrong hands and be cashed. They are not available in all currencies. It can also take time for a draft to be credited after presentation to the exporter's account. Oxfam Trading prefers not to use this method.

Payments for export consignments can be made only to the exporter, who raises the invoice. If a production unit is sending its goods through an exporter, then it is dependent on that exporter for settlement. The importer cannot bypass the exporter and pay directly to the producer.

It is possible to export handicrafts not against payment, but under a countertrade arrangement. This is where an importer sends goods of part or wholly equivalent value to the exporter. It can be useful to exporters who need to import equipment for their production.

Summary

1 International trade is regulated by procedures by which countries monitor and control their exports and imports. Products are identified by a classification code, by which they will be assessed for any restriction or liability for duty. The customs authority in each country controls exports and imports. There are essential documents which must pass from the exporting to the importing country. In order to obtain all the necessary documents and to clear consignments through customs quickly, most exporters and importers use specialist agents. Parcels sent by post also require standard documentation, unless they contain only samples of very small value.

2 There are four main methods of international transportation: air freight, sea freight, air post and sea post. Each has advantages and disadvantages, which need to be understood. Exporters should comply with instructions given by the importer unless there is a good reason to propose a change. Freight rates are often negotiable. Consignments are usually sent on the basis that the importer pays the freight bill. This facility is not available for post parcels. A freight consignment cannot be delivered until the importer or its agent has cleared it through customs.

3 Not only exporters, but also the government of the country of sale, want prompt and full payment for their exports. There are two main methods which offer security to the exporter that the importer will make proper payment, the letter of credit and documentary collection. It is not advisable to send documents to an importer without setting up a guaranteed payment system, unless it is a completely trustworthy customer. Importers will sometimes pay a proportion of the value of the order in advance. Money may be transferred internationally in a number of ways. A transfer between the importer's and exporter's bank account is the safest method, and it can be accomplished quickly by telex.

CONCLUSION

Ten Golden Rules ...
... for the exporter:

1   Confirm the customer's order promptly.

2   Advise your bank details and preferred method of payment.

3   Make the products as specified.

4   Follow the labelling and packaging instructions.

5   Impose strict quality control.

6   Pack the consignment adequately.

7   Meet the delivery date.

8   Despatch it by the method requested.

9   Send full and correct commercial documents.

10 Communicate any difficulties; clarify any uncertainties.

And one for the importer:

Make sure your orders are clear in all details and within the exporter's capacity to fulfil.

The number of very poor handicraft producers in the world is increasing, as new people start producing, in search of a source of income. If the handicraft sector is going to fulfil the hopes placed in it, marketing must assume its pre-eminent business role. Making the product is only the beginning; it is successfully selling it which counts. An understanding of the opportunities and problems of export marketing is vital to the success of handicraft producers, and this book is intended to help producers and exporters in their attempts to extend their markets and increase their sales, so that the people who make the handicrafts can receive a proper reward for their artistry and skill.

Notes and references

1. The four Ps of marketing were first defined by McCarthy, E.J., (1964) in *Basic Marketing: A Managerial Approach*, London: R.D.Irwin.

2. Ansoff, H.I. (1968), *Corporate Strategy*, London: Penguin.

3. For a critical appraisal of projects established to create income for poor people, see Hurley, D. (1990), *Income Generation Schemes for the Urban Poor*, Oxford: Oxfam.

4. Details of financial statements and calculations of costs and overheads are not dealt with in this book. The author's (1987), *Financial Management of a Small Handicraft Business*, Oxfam/Intermediate Technology Publications, might be helpful on these subjects, and also on pricing, which is dealt with in Chapter 7.3 here.

5. Quoted from Deschampsneuf, H. (1984), *Export for the Small Business*, London: Kogan Page.

6. This list was suggested by Copeland, M.T. (1924), *Principles of Merchandising*, London: A.W.Shaw, and re-presented by Waterworth, D. (1987), in *Marketing for the Small Business*, London: MacMillan.

   See also Chapter 6.1 on social concerns affecting the behaviour of consumers.

7. Quoted from Levitt, T. (1983), The Marketing Imagination, London: The Free Press.

8. A comprehensive brochure describing ITC's programmes was published in 1990 and is available free of charge. ITC publications are also free of charge for requests received from developing countries.

9. Quoted from ITC's brochure, p.22.

10. Quoted from UNESCO'S booklet describing the Ten-Year Plan of Action, p.3.

11. This description is generally agreed by members of the two associations of ATOs: the European Fair Trade Association and the International Federation for Alternative Trade.

12. Oxfam Trading accords to some of its trading partners a priority status, by virtue of their special types of support to the producers. It is these priority trading partners who receive a dividend, and first claim to our producer services programme. Money from this programme fund is made available to all suppliers, and also to many organisations which we want to support but from which we cannot buy for one reason or another.

13. 'Bridge' is the name which Oxfam Trading gives to its importing activity. It suggests the link between producers and consumers. Oxfam Trading also undertakes trade in products made in Great Britain for the purpose of raising funds for its parent charity, Oxfam.

14. This is known as the Bridge Development Fund. It is made up of any trading surpluses after the distribution of the dividend, plus an annual grant from Oxfam. The Fund is administered by Oxfam Trading.

15. Smith, A. (1976), *The Wealth of Nations*, Oxford: Oxford University Press.

16. Letter by Stephen Salmon, Project Director, Thai Payap Project, 17 August 1990.

17. I have copied this story from Katz, B. (1987), *Managing Export Marketing*, London: Gower Publishing.

18. Letter by Stephen Salmon, Project Director, Thai Payap Project, 18 May 1990.

19. Annual Report 1990, Presbyterian Handicrafts Centre, Cameroon.

20. This is extracted from a document which was produced by Kenya External Trade Authority, 4 October 1978.

21. Banking practice in documentary credits throughout the world is in accordance with the Uniform Customs and Practice for Documentary Credits established by the International Chamber of Commerce. This definition comes from ICC's Guide to Documentary Credit Operations, published as their Brochure No.305, which gives much more detailed information than is included here.

Addresses of organisations referred to in this book

Centre for the Development of Industry
rue de l'Industrie 28
B-1040 Brussels
Belgium
Tel: (02) 513.41.00   Fax: (02) 511.75.93   Telex: 61427

EFTA Stichting European Fair Trade Association
Witmakerstraat 10
6211 JB Maastricht
Netherlands
Tel: (43) 256917   Fax: (43) 218820 att. EFTA   Telex: 59048

Intermediate Technology Publications Ltd
103-105 Southampton Row
London WC1B 4HH
United Kingdom
Tel: (071) 436 2013   Fax: (071) 436 2013   Telex: 268312

International Chamber of Commerce
38 Cours Albert 1er
75008 Paris
France
Tel: (1) 49 53 28 28 Fax: (1) 42 25 86 63 Telex: 650770

The International Federation for Alternative Trade
P.O.Box 2703
100 CS Amsterdam
Netherlands
Tel: (20) 27 25 66   Fax: (20) 27 70 34   Telex: 16119

International Labour Office,
4 route des Morillons,
1211 Geneva 22,
Switzerland.
Tel: (22) 799 6111 Fax: (22) 798 86 85 Telex: 415647

International Trade Centre UNCTAD/GATT
Palais des Nations
1211 Geneva 10
Switzerland
Tel: (22) 7300111   Fax: (22) 733 4439   Telex: 28 90 52

Oxfam Trading
Murdock Road
Bicester
Oxon OX6 7RF
United Kingdom
Tel: (0869) 245011   Fax: (0869) 247348   Telex: 838930

Traidcraft plc
Kingsway
Gateshead
Tyne & Wear NE11 0NE
United Kingdom
Tel:(091) 491 0591   Fax: (091) 482 2690   Telex: 53585

United Nations Educational, Scientific and Cultural Organisation
7 place de Fontenoy
75700 Paris
France
Tel: (1) 45 68 1000   Fax: (1) 45 67 16 90   Telex: 204461

Further reading

It is worthwhile to look at books on the theory and practice of marketing, and on export marketing in particular. They can help you to think about your own marketing mix. The only book I know which is specifically about export marketing of handicrafts is currently out of print:

Dembitzer, B. (1983), *Marketing Handicraft from Developing Countries.*

A valuable basic guide to procedures for exports from developing countries is provided by:

Allen, R. (ed.) (1983), *Exporting to the UK*, prepared by the United Kingdom Trade Agency for Developing Countries (now retitled the Developing Countries Trade Agency), 69 Cannon Street, London EC4N 5AB, Oxford: Pergamon Press.

A detailed treatment of the organisation of trade fairs which might be valuable to an exporter thinking of participating in one is:

(1974), *Exhibitor's Guide - Fairs, Salons, Exhibitions*, published by The Commission of European Communities, rue de la Loi 200, B-1049 Brussels, Belgium.

A number of agencies which are not major publishers have produced training manuals for use by small businesses. The ones listed below are those I have come across. Oxfam Trading would be interested in receiving copies of others which have been prepared. We are also planning to produce a series of short manuals which present some of the topics covered in this book in a more accessible fashion for inexperienced or new export businesses.

Hughes, J. (1981), *Guide for Exporters of Pacific Island Crafts*, London: Commonwealth Secretariat, Marlborough House, Pall Mall, London SW1.Prepared for a seminar on the Development of Artefacts and Handicrafts for Commonwealth Developing countries in the Pacific Region, organised by the Export Market Division of the Commonwealth Secretariat in collaboration with the Government of Papua New Guinea and the South Pacific Bureau for Economic Co-operation.

'Marketing: What it is and Why it's Important for Women', *Newsletter* 31, 1985, New York: International Women's Tribune Centre Inc., 777 United Nations Plaza, New York 10017, USA.

(1985), *The Business of Small Business*, Saint Paul: Women's Economic Development Corporation, 1885 University Avenue West, Suite 395, Saint Paul, Minnesota 55105.

(1983), *Marketing Hints for Jamaican Craft Workers*, Kingston, Jamaica: Things Jamaican and Inter-American Institute for Co-operation in Agriculture (IICA) P.O.Box 349, Kingston 6, Jamaica.

A series of three manuals for small business training in Jamaica:

(1986), *Starting and Financing a Small Business in Jamaica;*
(1986), *Marketing Jamaican Small Business Products;*
(1985), *Operating a Small Business in Jamaica - A Guide,* Kingston, Jamaica: IICA.

Malick, S.(1985), *Planning Income and Employment Generation for Rural Women — The Marketing Approach,* Geneva: International Labour Organization (ILO).

MATCOM is an ILO project, started in 1978, which designs and publishes material for training managers and which supports programmes to improve co-operative training and the training of trainers. For example :

A Handicraft Co-operative — Management. One of a series within MATCOM — Materials and Techniques for Co-operative Management Training — ILO, 1987

Kundervatter, S., *Marketing Strategy, Training Activities for Entrepreneurs,* Washington: OEF International, 1815H Street, NW, 11th Floor, Washington DC 20006, USA.

Mercadeo, Elementos de Economica, Contabilidad para Artesanos and Procesos Productivos. A series of four manuals for training in business management by Artesanias de Colombia/ Museo de Artes y Tradiciones Populares, Apartado Aereo 10776, Bogota, Colombia.

Your Business Success, Durham Small Business Club Limited, West Pelton House, West Pelton, Nr. Chester-le-Street, Co. Durham, DH9 6SG, England. This is a training manual, available in three versions according to type of business, for businesses in Britain. Section A of Version No. 1 is particularly helpful on planning in a new business.

Packaging of Handicrafts, Kenya External Trade Authority, P.O.Box 43137, Nairobi, Kenya.

INDEX

183